YOU THROW LIKE A GIRL

THE BLIND SPOT OF MASCULINITY

DON McPHERSON

EDGE
OF SPORTS

You Throw Like a Girl is the latest title in Dave Zirin's **Edge of Sports** imprint. Addressing issues across many different sports at both the professional and nonprofessional/collegiate level, Edge of Sports aims to provide an even deeper articulation of the daily collision between sports and politics, giving cutting-edge writers the opportunity to fully explore their areas of expertise in book form.

Published by Akashic Books
©2019 Don McPherson

Paperback ISBN: 978-1-61775-705-1
Hardcover ISBN: 978-1-61775-779-2
Library of Congress Control Number: 2019935373
All rights reserved

Edge of Sports
c/o Akashic Books
Brooklyn, New York, USA
Ballydehob, Co. Cork, Ireland
Twitter: @AkashicBooks
Facebook: AkashicBooks
E-mail: info@akashicbooks.com
Website: www.akashicbooks.com

With gratitude for Margaret and Gene,
and hope for Ava and Liza

Table of Contents

Introduction   9

Chapter One: Black Man with Privilege   25
Chapter Two: Twenty-Nine   52
Chapter Three: Hyperbole and Myth   75
Chapter Four: Be a Man   100
Chapter Five: You Throw Like a Girl   121
Chapter Six: A Men's Issue   140
Chapter Seven: Traditions of Silence   166
Chapter Eight: The "Streets" in the Pocket   188

Conclusion: Be Your Son's Father, Not Your Father's Son   206

Introduction

OPRAH

I always knew one day I'd be a guest on *The Oprah Winfrey Show*.

By most accounts, I've lived a charmed life. I was an all-American athlete in high school and college, played seven years of professional football, and was inducted into the College Football Hall of Fame. I come from a solid, closely knit family, the youngest of five children; my two brothers were also professional athletes.

Being on *Oprah* was consistent with my life's trajectory. But, just as my life as an athlete was beyond my dreams, I also never imagined the subject matter that would bring me to her stage.

I had been invited onto the show to discuss my work of engaging men to prevent men's violence against women. It was a moment of great irony because it was a rebuke of that which made my life as an athlete special. I was an anomaly among men, confronting and dismantling myths about masculinity and sports—the very things that had lavished me with privilege— and I was there to tell Oprah why this was an essential process for ending all forms of men's violence against women.

My appearance on the show was, in many ways, the vision of my mentor and friend Jackson Katz, who joined me on the show. When I retired from professional football I worked with

Jackson, a pioneering voice on masculinity and the issue of men's violence against women. One of the fundamental goals of his work was to challenge existing ideas of masculinity while encouraging men with social status (like athletes) to normalize the conversation and help prevent violence against women.

I wish taking such a stance had been enough to effect real change, but it wasn't. *The Oprah Winfrey Show* was not the optimal venue to concretely deliver the message fundamental to ending men's violence against women. Nor was simply dismantling my privilege the answer.

I arrived at Harpo Studios a few hours before taping the show and spent most of the time anxiously pacing the green room that was at the end of a long hallway. The early morning silence was broken when a familiar voice, from the other end of the hallway, called out, "It's the *O Magazine* man!" It was an enthusiastic and iconic tone heard frequently gifting extravagant surprises to exuberant audiences and calling the names of Hollywood's most famous stars. It was surreal to see Oprah Winfrey walking toward me with a welcoming smile. She had just finished her morning workout and walked into the green room with a towel over her shoulder, wearing sweatpants and sneakers and, most notably, no airs or pretense. Her presence was overwhelming and yet she was warm and engaging, just what you would expect from someone who has had such a profound and indelible impact on American culture.

When I walked onstage at *The Oprah Winfrey Show* on September 23, 2002, I did so confident in my privileged masculinity and fully aware of how I had attained it. I was seven years removed from my professional football career, and over that time I had been immersed in engaging men on the complexities of masculinity and raising societal awareness of men's violence against women. But I was not a confident activist nor a spokesman for masculinity. I was a scared boy hiding behind the facade of cool toughness I had cultivated my entire life as a football player, and now I was trying to use that facade to face questions most men ignored.

I have a clear memory of how that facade was formed. At eight years old, I first attempted to play football. I was the third son and my two older brothers were stars of their age group in our town. I walked onto the field assuming that I would extend the family legacy; I felt as if all eyes were on my every move and that I had to live up to expectations. Anxiously, I stood in line with other boys, determined to catch the ball being thrown at me once it was my turn. But the anxiety was too much to bear and instead of running out to catch a pass, I ran to the parking lot.

The following year, at age nine, I tried again. This time the scrutiny of being a "McPherson boy" was heightened by the fact that my performance, or lack thereof the previous year, was still fresh in everyone's mind—especially my own. This time the drill was a simple handoff and weave through a few cones in the grass. The second attempt ended like the first, with me crying and running off the field to my father's car, in clear sight of our town's entire football community. Compared to the success of my brothers, it was clear that I was quickly becoming a colossal embarrassment. My father gave up trying and I found myself on my own; I had to muster the courage to overcome the cowardice I had readily displayed.

At age ten, I unleashed a talent that usurped my fears. But football did not erase my fears; it was merely the platform that enabled me to demonstrate the kind of masculinity that could disguise my most paralyzing fear—vulnerability. I was not fearful of the game of football; I loved to play it. But the *performance* of masculinity and the inherent expectations that

I should ignore and disguise my fears, vulnerabilities, and insecurities—that part I had to learn.

For nineteen years, football would provide the stage upon which I mastered the performance of masculinity. In public I thrived, portraying an aloof indifference and proclivity for subtle yet discernible heterosexist attitudes and behaviors. However, internally I struggled with the truth of my dichotomous existence. As I progressed as a football player, the performance grew more grotesque and morphed into absurdity. I achieved social status without being a very social person, with privileges and perks that I neither wanted nor deserved; the respect I received bordered on "fear" that my (violent) physicality was a foreboding force simmering in my persona; I received attention (especially from women and "important" men) that afforded me consideration and inclusion in places from which I would have otherwise been excluded. I became a caricature of privileged masculinity, a "real man"—successful, but living by a set of false ideals that belied my authentic identity. Intuitively I understood this, but the privilege it afforded, and the same fears that haunted the ten-year-old me, kept me from thoroughly exploring or dismantling my public persona. I had become comfortable in the myth.

While the Oprah experience was incomparable, it did little to achieve and sustain the ultimate goal of my work: to proactively engage and enlist men in preventing men's violence against women. The approach is rooted in promoting positive conversations with men to expand the fundamental understanding of masculinity, defining it in ways that are affirming but do not perpetuate patriarchy, misogyny, sexism, and violence against women.

At that time, I was trying to find a publisher for what would eventually become this book. During a commercial break, I told

Oprah about my book and she immediately responded with the name of a publisher. Within hours of my flight landing at home in New York, I reached out to that publisher and name-dropped one of the most famous and influential human beings on the planet. The manuscript was in the mail the next morning. I was certain that with Oprah's recommendation, the book would be on its way to publication.

The book was quickly rejected. I was told that Oprah's audience didn't need it to understand the issue, and men, for whom this book was ultimately written, would not purchase it. It was a profound rebuff I was not ready to accept at the time. And I found the response to be sexist and condescending—not to women, but to men. I believed then, as I do now, that men *do* care about being better sons, husbands, and fathers. I believe men *do* want to confront the issue of violence against women.

Still, nearly two decades since that appearance on *Oprah*, I have come to terms with the fact that in a certain respect the publisher was right. Men generally don't care to have this discussion. What has been haunting me is, why? What is keeping men from participating in this conversation of addressing one of the most intimate and widespread problems in our society? If masculinity is about being courageous and tough, why are men afraid to engage this conversation? Most importantly, what is keeping men from talking about how to be better fathers to their sons?

THE SOCIALIZATION OF BOYS

When I first began this work, shortly after retiring from football at age twenty-nine, I probed my life for lessons that instilled in me what it means to be a man. None of what I found was positive or affirming. What I unearthed was shaming language, bravado, and stoic posturing. That's when I arrived at the quintessential insult to boys: "You throw like a girl." It succinctly illustrates the foundation of men's violence against women: the belief that girls and women are "less than" and the unspoken suppression of boys' emotional wholeness.

The more I asked the question, "What does it mean to *be a man?*" the more salient and important that insult became in confronting misogyny and sexism's direct link to violence against women. In fact, it led to a deeper, inescapable truth that *we do not raise boys to be men, we raise them* not *to be women—or gay men.*

In examining this profound truth over recent decades, I am troubled to have found that we raise boys expecting them to devalue girls; it's an absolute requirement of being male. Eventually, "You throw like a girl" became more than a framework for my lectures and led to critical follow-up questions: How do we raise boys to be whole men without degrading our daughters in the process? How do we change the narrative about what it means to be a man? How do we get men to understand that being a "real man" and a "whole man" are not mutually exclusive identities?

It is important to note that I write as a cisgender heterosexual man aimed at reaching other cis heterosexual men. This focus is not meant to exclude nonconforming individuals but to identify and examine the trenchant dogma of masculinity that leads to men's violence against women, and the impact this narrow understanding of masculinity has on the healthy development of boys.

Throughout this book I use the word "masculinity," even though it is too often used as a monolithic term for the characteristics of men. More broadly, the term "masculinities" accurately accounts for the differences between and among men, yet we must acknowledge that we do not deliberately nurture boys as whole beings who are impacted by and possess a wide array of gendered qualities. Instead, we give them rigid commands and demand they conform to a strict set of behaviors and beliefs, which comprise what I call the *mandate, performance, promise,* and *lie* of masculinity. Together, these four tenets, which I will explore in the following chapters, constitute the dogma of masculinity—the expectations of male behavior and how it can earn for men the privileges of a patriarchal culture. Men are expected to categorically accept this privilege without understanding how or why it's achieved. *How do men understand privilege they have not earned? If male privilege comes at the expense of women, is it truly privilege (and does it belong to men?) or is it more accurately defined as oppression?*

#METOO

To engage with these questions about privilege means to get directly involved in the gender issues of the day. And if men needed a reason to get involved, we certainly got one in 2017. Arguably one of the most significant cultural awakenings of our time, #MeToo, started by Tarana Burke in 2006, became a global movement in 2017, when more than a dozen women in Hollywood came forward with allegations of sexual abuse against film mogul Harvey Weinstein. Subsequently, millions of women used their voices to reveal how they too had been sexually assaulted and abused yet had chosen silence over retribution, public shame, or loss of professional opportunity. This was reminiscent of a public conversation a few years earlier emerging from Janay Palmer's decision to marry NFL player Ray Rice, despite his highly publicized physical assault of her just a few weeks prior. A globally trending hashtag, #WhyIStayed, gave voice to women around the world, inviting them to lament why they stayed in abusive relationships with men who routinely hurt them. However, in this case, as with #MeToo, one voice in the discussion was glaringly absent—that of men, *all* men.

These conversations and movements are opportunities for our participation, but our proper role is not clear. What should men be doing? As a man, in the aftermath of violence, I feel I can only offer support, condolences, and sympathy. Truthfully, even empathy is so grossly insufficient that it feels disingenuous and unproductive. The only way this becomes a productive conversation is if we also ask, very pointedly, *why?* And truly seek to understand and make real change to the culture that creates perpetrators. *If we are going to ask why she stays, should we not also explore why* he *stays as well? Why does he commit the violence and abuse his position of power? Is not the abuse of power an acknowledgment of assumed innate power over women? Can addressing the issue of violence address this question, or is deeper examination required?*

It's important to note the ways in which we systematically avoid the common denominator in nearly all societal violence—men. The violence committed by athletes like Ray Rice fits a familiar narrative of violent black men or entitled athletes. Similarly, the sexual abuse and misconduct by powerful and wealthy men like Weinstein, TV journalist Charlie Rose, Matt Lauer, Russell Simmons, Garrison Keillor, numerous members of the US Congress, and a whole slew of others is so commonplace that their cover-ups and "hush money" are held in greater disdain than their original crimes against women. In each case, we fail to examine masculinity. We simply look away.

When Jackson Katz began talking to me about the issue of men's violence against women, he was adamant about including the word "men's." The point was to emphasize men's role in committing the violence as well as the essential role men can play in preventing it. We should no longer consider this a

"woman's issue" but a "men's issue." But how is it a men's issue? And how do we engage men in a sustained dialogue about
"men's violence"?

MEN AS ALLIES

I've realized the key to drawing men into a sustained dialogue
lies in adopting a more aspirational approach to discussing
masculinity. We need to be *for* positive outcomes, not simply
against bad things that have occurred. This is why I've long
doubted the efficacy of prevention programs, dating back to
when I first began working on social issues in college for a New
York State program called Athletes Against Drunk Driving.
Such programs are typically aimed at preventing the last horrific incident from reoccurring, but progress and growth come
by proactively teaching and instilling processes that promote
positive outcomes.

There are many negative terms to describe masculinity
("privileged," "hegemonic," "toxic," "violent") as well as ways
to address it. (We must "redefine manhood," "confront toxic
masculinity," "challenge patriarchy and male privilege.") None
of these constructions are positive and they only condemn the
fundamental way in which men's identity is formed and lived.
Furthermore, this language might only exacerbate men's defen-
siveness on gender issues.

I believe we need to engage men in a new set of terms
that are aspirational and more accurately representative of the
wholeness of men. Our approach needs to be deliberate and
intentional. We can no longer allow good guys to be defined by
the nobility of emotional abstinence or those who do not con-
sciously harm others. We must be aspirational and courageous
as we raise future generations of boys to be emotionally whole
and fully actualized men. If we do this honestly and coura-

geously, we will find the depths of our humanity: vulnerability, fear, insecurity, and love. We will discover that we care deeply, fear viscerally, and love irrationally. But we will also see very clearly how we deliberately and systematically stifle this truth simply to uphold something we have never truly acknowledged or questioned: how masculinity is governed by the dogma of patriarchy.

Although understanding masculinity has increasingly become a part of the work to end men's violence against women, it continues to lack the priority I believe is necessary for sustainable cultural change. That work is informed and directed by the experiences of women who have survived men's violence and those who advocate for all women and their rights to safety and equity. Men are enlisted by women with a set of priorities strictly aimed at eradicating the culture and behaviors of men that harm women's lives. Underlying this strategy is an appeal to men's sense of duty and protection of women. I refer to this as "protective patriarchy": a noble sense of male identity that comes from our prescribed roles as protectors and providers.

As men working in the "prevention" field, we often refer to our role as "allies" to women who need to remain accountable to women. We are allies because our charge is defined by the experience of women and it is at the behest and beseeching of women. Therefore, our role is in support of their work and their perspective. While we ultimately endeavor to engage men, this dynamic, in many ways, distances us from men. Since men don't voluntarily come to this discussion, there is an inherent loss of accountability to and solidarity with them. Male "allies" are challenged to remain steadfast and unwavering in the protection and advancement of women's lives and rights while finding solidarity in a cultural environment in which those rights are regularly violated. This is where accountability to women can cloud men's authenticity: sensing the urgent imperative to confront violence, we seize upon the rare moments to engage men but ignore their complexity. We want men to use their protective "instincts" while ignoring the fact that protective patriarchy is not instinctual but rather a product of a set of learned behaviors that narrowly define masculinity.

To sincerely and authentically engage men, we must have an honest conversation about masculinity. Failing to talk about it makes us less capable of thoroughly understanding or actualizing our roles as allies to women. This is especially true when deconstructing the issue of violence. Violence is used to control that which we refuse to understand or are incapable of fully understanding. If men don't understand the complexities and wholeness of masculinity, we will never comprehend our full humanity and therefore will use violence to control the environment and people around us who do not conform to our narrow view of ourselves and the world. If we do not work to understand the intricacies that influence male behavior (including violence), then we will be reduced to confronting men's violence no differently than women have attempted to dismantle male privilege. Or, worse, we will perpetuate the use of violence and force as the solution.

ACCOUNTABILITY VS. CHIVALRY

Most men will quickly and readily agree that violence against women is wrong and that something should be done to stop it. Some men will only assume such a stance to appear politically correct or to offer up a predictable vigilante-style bravado. Other men are truly sincere and act out of a sense of deep caring or hurt from having witnessed firsthand some form of violence against a loved one. However, what men do not always want to deal with is a solution that demands scrutiny of their own behavior and privilege, even in the context of doing what they know is right. So when the topic turns from the problem they can "see" in others to the problem they ignore in themselves, they become rigid and reticent. In other words, when they have to be accountable to themselves as opposed to chivalrous to women, men feel incriminated. The pushback is immediate. This is the blind spot of masculinity: the defense of narrowly defined masculinity that keeps us from exploring and living a more whole, complete version of ourselves. *How do we move beyond the protective patriarchy that brings them to the discussion to a more fulfilling conversation about the wholeness of masculinity?*

To authentically and truthfully process this question, we must first consider the way in which men are taught to care for girls and women. In other words, to truly be accountable to women and confront the core elements of misogyny and sexism, we must relinquish the mythical intent of chivalry—the protection of women. This would strip away the notion that women need the violent, obstinate, and overbearing qualities of male power and privilege for their protection and purpose. We must do this not because women implore us to do so, but because we truly care about the healthy wholeness of boys and men.

THE PIVOT

The approach must focus on helping men become better men. In most life endeavors, we work and train to attain excellence, not just success in the moment; in sports and academics, we work toward excellence, not the prevention of failure. Moreover, we do not train for victory by a discernible margin but mastery of a discipline or performance. We must apply the same vigor for excellence when considering the ideology of masculinity.

That is why I believe there must be a "pivot," a shift in

the conversation *from* what women have asked men to do and *toward* a more trenchant, robust, and sustained conversation among men about the aspirational and essential values of masculinity. This must occur devoid of assertions of culpability for violence against women and focus intensely and intently on nurturing purposeful, healthy, and whole masculinity. We should be asking more what boys and men can become and asking less about what they should or shouldn't do.

This pivot should in no way perpetuate or defend the privilege of masculinity or advance the arcane creed of patriarchy. Nor should it attempt to diminish the work to end men's violence against women or come at the expense of the struggle for gender equality. In fact, gender equality can *only* be achieved if men acknowledge we have a gendered identity and fully understand why and how gender matters in our lives. This requires a thorough and honest interrogation of masculinity, which, when fully understood, will reveal the complexity of our gendered identity and the core elements of the misogyny and sexism that lead to men's violence against women. While we remain accountable to women, we are also responsible for the next generation of boys for whom we are obligated to lead in a better way than our fathers led us.

The nuances of masculinity are not something that men regularly, if ever, seek to understand. In fact, most men don't feel they *own* masculinity. We want to own "being a man" or "manhood," but not the broad complexities and dilemmas of masculinity. We have been sold on the belief that our behavior (good or bad) is "just the way men are." Even when a man does bad things, we defend him saying, "He's a good man and just made a mistake." This is the adult version of "boys will be boys": the excuse we make for the abhorrent behavior we are privileged to choose to ignore. This is the epitome of the blind spot. By default, we accept the "inevitability of male violence." We often have difficulty considering or articulating how we as men see ourselves in a broad spectrum or context. This is partly what leads to a lack of self-analysis, exploration, and growth: the unexamined belief that masculinity is a "fixed" thing. *What is the process by which men learn such hardened and diminished understandings of themselves? And how do we engage men in a way that enables a broader, more fluid understanding of masculinity?*

MY FATHER

Just after midnight on August 9, 2013, I received a call from my sister in San Diego. My father had suffered a stroke and was in a coma. By dawn I was on a flight from New York. When my brother-in-law Mike met me at the airport, he prepared me for the scene awaiting me at the hospital. When he cautioned that my father was in a coma and unable to speak, I thought, *Huh, I just spent the past five hours in deep conversation with him.* His voice in my head was more powerful than his DNA in my blood; it was like a second consciousness. Intellectually and emotionally, I had carried on a dialogue with him that was warm and intimate. When Mike said that he could not speak, I knew I was there to say goodbye to his body and that the man he had been was still alive in me.

My father was a great man. He also personified the word "stoic." As I spent time with him in his final days, I marveled at how he instilled in me so much of who he was, though he said very little and emoted even less. On the plane ride, I thought of him from my perspective as an adult, recalling our most recent conversations. But once in his presence, despite his inanimate state, I became a boy, his child, and I was brought back to the moment I first understood our bond. It was a beautiful Saturday in the late summer of 1977, when unexpected visitors arrived at our house. I was not in the mood for company and retreated to my room. The door was locked. Frantically, I pounded the door, and slowly it crept open. My father retreated with a look of surrender on his face. He had gotten the word about our visitors much earlier and was prepared to sit them out with a few newspapers and a nap. What he hadn't anticipated was my company. For that matter, I didn't expect his.

That day in my room was one of the greatest memories of my childhood with my father. There I was, in this silent and profound moment, with the person who would ultimately have the greatest impact on the man I would someday become. We sat, read, and slept in relative silence, yet shared so much of what we had in common, the stoic expression of father-and-son love.

When he passed away, I thought a lot more about that silence, that discerning and prideful quality that was passed from *his* dad to my brothers and me. *What messages and lessons did I have to "infer" or seek elsewhere for a more complete and thorough understanding, because he simply did not talk? And what power did his silence give to other influences in my life—coaches, other men, the media—that shaped the way I conveyed the mandate of masculinity?*

My father's stoicism made him an enigma to me, which by extension made *me* an enigma. Though our relationship was loving, it lacked intentional direction regarding my growth toward a whole, loving masculinity. Invariably and perhaps unwittingly, in his reticence he acquiesced to a prevailing understanding of masculinity shaped by a culture of men with little interest in my wholeness as a person. I always took my father's stoicism as the epitome of tough masculinity and, since it was respected by other men, as something regal and noble. Not until later in my life did I realize it was also incomplete.

I aspire to live my life in the new toughness of masculinity—deliberate, intentional, loving, caring, egalitarian, and nonviolent. All the things my father was but was incapable of articulating. I believe it's time for us as men to expand the definition of what it means to be men, understand the complexities of our gender, and learn to be loving, caring, and whole as we raise the next generation of boys to be loving, caring, and whole.

Black Man with Privilege

ICONIC MASCULINITY

It was just before seven p.m. on a Tuesday evening in early December 2008. I stood in a room adjacent to the grand ballroom of the famed Waldorf Astoria hotel in New York City, about to be introduced to a crowd of seventeen hundred guests in attendance for the College Football Hall of Fame induction ceremonies. Backstage, our grand entrance was prepared: the Hall of Famers enter first, followed by members of the five-tiered dais (which included venerable dignitaries from the worlds of football, media, military service, politics, and business), and finally the incoming Hall of Fame class. I had been asked to deliver remarks on behalf of the entire class—a role I considered an extraordinary honor. The hard part of the evening was having to contain the little boy in me, feeling in awe of the men in the room and riddled with insecurity and the thought that I did not belong among that incredible collection of football players and dignitaries.

At one point, while chatting with legendary NFL players Ronnie Lott and Lynn Swann, I made brief eye contact with Senator John Glenn and we exchanged a knowing smile. Earlier in the evening, Senator Glenn and I had met and talked about both football and his mission as the sole astronaut aboard *Friendship 7,* which made him the first American to orbit the earth. I'm sure he's told the story more times than the miles he's traveled in space, but for me it was a rare and prodigious moment. I was not the only person personally inspired by him— the entire world had stood still as he explored the outer limits of our universe. But that night, our names were on the same page of the evening's program as fellow honorees.

Each year the living history of college football descends upon New York for the National Football Foundation's College Hall of Fame induction dinner, honoring the very best of the game's past and present. In addition to inducting a new class of Hall of Famers, the dinner recognizes a group of student-athletes who excel in the classroom as well as on the field. It also recognizes great Americans whose lives have been shaped by the game of football. Honorees have included some of the most iconic and influential men of twentieth-century American history: Army generals Douglas MacArthur and Norman Schwarzkopf, presidents Eisenhower, Kennedy, Ford, and Reagan, Supreme Court justices, as well as Bob Hope, John Wayne, and Jackie Robinson. And on this night, I stood in that legacy with Mercury astronaut and senator John Glenn.

At the time, it seemed surreal because I never considered that my success as a football player could warrant association with such men. I marveled at how the game I had played on the streets of my neighborhood as a child brought me into proximity with them. At the same time, however, I did not question that the game of football was an integral component of iconic American leadership and masculinity. All of us on that stage had many significant influences in our lives, but none was more celebrated and considered more foundational to our success than our participation in football. All of our schools produced students as accomplished in their fields as the athletes were— some more so—but few alumni can bring that level of collective pride and pageantry to their institutions. The lofty mantel upon which we athletes sit is often undeserved, but it reflects an American nostalgia from which sports cannot be extracted. I think of this often when considering the profound role football played in my life, providing me the opportunity to attend Syracuse University, which led to innumerable advantages and privileges I would never have had otherwise. The Hall of Fame dinner was a grandiose exclamation point on a life of privilege the sport allowed me to enjoy.

TRANSCENDENT PRIVILEGE

The opulent Waldorf Astoria could not have been more removed from the football culture and the world in which I was raised. Each year, the moment after the dinner has concluded and I step into the streets of New York City, pulling my hat down firmly against the December wind, I am transformed. Instantly, I am reminded of my father, who was a detective with the New York Police Department for more than thirty years before retiring from the Internal Affairs Division. I always understood his stoic demeanor as a tool of survival as he managed the tensions of being both a black police officer *and* a cop who investigated bad cops. Neither was a popular identity in New York in the 1970s.

He is always on my mind when I am in the city, because his work and sacrifice made it a better place for me. In fact, that evening I was inducted was special and profound for him as well. At that point retired more than twenty years, he returned to New York to attend the dinner and stay overnight as a guest in the Waldorf Astoria. He believed in the promise of progress, and through his son witnessed its realization, enabled by the game of football.

That 2008 Hall of Fame dinner was a sign that, in many

ways, I lived through an interesting period of social change and my understanding of my privilege was just beginning. Several years later, on the day following the 2014 Hall of Fame dinner, I would be recognized again—this time for my work to prevent men's violence against women. And again, and even more poignantly, I was struck by how life and my sense of privilege were evolving. I left the Waldorf to travel across town and join my fellow honorees, one of whom was then–vice president of the United States Joe Biden.

December 10, 2014, was International Human Rights Day, and the day the Vital Voices Global Partnership held its inaugural Voices of Solidarity Awards dinner. Vital Voices is a global NGO (nongovernmental organization) founded in 1997 by then–First Lady Hillary Clinton and Secretary of State Madeleine Albright. Vital Voices empowers and invests in women's leadership throughout the world. Vice President Biden and I were joined by actor and activists Sir Patrick Stewart and Bafana Khumalo, cofounder of Sonke Gender Justice, an organization that works on gender and social justice issues across Africa, as the first recipients to be recognized for our "solidarity." It was a tremendous honor to be associated with Vital Voices and Joe, Patrick, and Bafana.

Following my remarks from the podium, as I left the stage, I passed Vice President Biden's table and said hello to him and to his wife Jill. When I got back to my table someone asked if that was the first time I'd met the vice president, to which I replied with a prideful smile, "Who, *Joe*?" It was not our first meeting. In fact, we were more than familiar and share a bond of "solidarity" more significant than the recognition we received that evening: we are fellow alums of Syracuse University.

I first met Joe Biden on a basketball court in Delaware. It

was just after my rookie season with the Philadelphia Eagles and I was playing on our off-season basketball team. We barnstormed throughout southeastern Pennsylvania, Delaware, and south Jersey, playing high school faculty, fire departments, and local "all-stars" for charity. At one such game, on the campus of the University of Delaware, I met Senator Biden during pregame warm-ups. He promptly let me know that for this game he was representing his alma mater, University of Delaware, but that he had received his law degree from Syracuse. We enjoyed a few laughs, fondly reminiscing about Syracuse and sharing the compulsory jokes about the dreadful winters there. We then played an awful basketball game for a good cause.

Years later, following my retirement from football, I began working in the field to prevent all forms of men's violence against women. This work frequently brought me to Washington, DC, to testify before congressional committees, work with the Departments of Justice and Education, and support various legislation written to establish and strengthen laws that protect women and their rights. One such piece of legislation was the 1994 Violence Against Women Act, sponsored by Senator Biden.

On several occasions, I attended meetings or events with Senator Biden. Those moments had the gravity of an issue greater than each of us. Still, the source of our bond remained our alma mater and the unyielding loyalty that many college alumni share with each other. I was always proud of my alma mater; it was a piece of my identity as significant as family, culture, religion, or community. But I was also humbled to know that had it not been for football, I would not have had the opportunity to attend Syracuse University and have life-changing affiliations with people like the former vice president.

As a high school student, my successes as an athlete began

to shape and expand my options. I had the privilege of choosing what college I would attend, which included having my pick of school environment, educators, and coaches. As a young black man in 1983, it was indeed a unique and privileged position in which I found myself. That opportunity not only expanded my life's options; I also earned a position for which I had little understanding and hadn't even intended to achieve.

PRIVILEGE SUPPLANTS IDENTITY

Football helped me transcend much of the racism my father routinely faced in his life. Race was always a subtle backdrop to how he observed my life experiences and those of my siblings. Football did more than provide the opportunity to avoid institutional racism and the obstacles it posed to upward social, economic, and professional mobility. In many ways, for me it guaranteed a certain level of transcendence. Earning a scholarship to attend Syracuse meant neither my family nor I felt the pressure of the onerous cost of higher education. Beyond playing football, I was not driven by particular academic interests so, ironically, I had the freedom to intellectually explore and truly "soul search" as a student.

As quarterback of the team, I was not just a leader on the field but also expected to represent the team in so many other ways, such as in the media and the community. For some of my teammates this was a hassle, but I loved being in the community and began using my status to talk with kids about important social issues and making good decisions in life. This kept me grounded as I was processing my own life decisions and trying to identify myself outside of that which gave me status. I enjoyed giving more depth to the identity of a college football player—removing the helmet and sharing who I really was as a person. I loved the freedom my position gave me to confidently express my idiosyncratic ways despite knowing that all that really mattered to those around me was winning football games. But something else was happening. Notwithstanding my incessant attempts to humanize my identity, as I gained more success as a football player I increasingly became a caricature, a one-dimensional image defined by my physicality and ability to perform in the game. When that image consumed the entirety of my identity, I became a "thing" that represented every stereotype of a male athlete: interested only in the game, my physicality, and my performance—unfeeling, impervious to pain, and the embodiment of violent masculinity. Moreover, the caricature existed in constant performance for the benefit and gaze of fans, especially men. The expectations of me as a man began to narrow and wane. *Who* I was was progressively diminished by *what* I was.

As I ventured into the business realm of the NFL, my identity shrunk even further, as I became a commodity with a very short shelf life. The demands to maximize commercial potential in that environment were not conducive to any sort of self-reflection, which would theoretically distract a player from the game and jeopardize the urgent imperative that he remain prepared to compete. From the outside, there were few social levers to encourage personal growth; the narrowness of my identity was assumed and even celebrated by a society that only valued my athletic pedigree.

We all experience this as athletes, and we also know that society's celebration of our prowess will inevitably come to an end. We do all we can to postpone that moment, even if it costs us some piece of our identity. I played professionally in the NFL and Canadian Football League for seven years, all the while cognizant of that inevitable fall from grace, yet ignoring my personal growth as a man.

As a young man in college, I struggled with that shrinking identity and the isolation I felt as fame (and privilege) became a reality that I was reluctant to accept. Still, I began to realize its purpose—to allow me the platform to work with young people on social issues, in a unique and powerful way. In every conversation with young people I listened intently, ever wary that my life's station was a subtle impediment to effective communication. As I matured, the rift between their perception of me and my true identity as a person widened dramatically. It wasn't a function of my age and the generational divide between us— there was something deeper going on, and I was about to find out what it was.

EPIPHANY

The most frequent question people ask me is, what inspired or led to my work in the field of sexual and domestic violence prevention? Was I a perpetrator or survivor? Was I raised by a "pack" of feminist women (like the proverbial boy raised by wolves)? Or was there some traumatic experience to which I was responding, using the work as a source of cathartic healing?

It was none of those things. Although there was a healing process, it would be years before I would truly understand it. But there was one pivotal moment that compelled me to examine my identity and the social force from which my privilege was derived.

I began my career of talking with young people on social issues in 1984 as a sophomore at Syracuse with a program called Athletes Against Drunk Driving (AADD). It was a statewide program in New York that placed prominent athletes onstage and in classrooms alongside state law enforcement officers to address issues of drunk driving and underage drinking. Everything about the program appealed to me: there was a sense of mission, a critical issue to address, and a need to reach a vulnerable population. Most importantly, it allowed me the latitude to bring my voice and personal narrative to each engagement. I honestly did not have a discernible philosophy or message, yet I loved the process of finding my authentic voice and learning how to make my story part of an inspiring and educational experience for students.

During my rookie season with the Philadelphia Eagles in 1988, I continued working with AADD, primarily on Long Island where I grew up. Through that work I connected with Warren Breining, who along with administering AADD on Long Island had founded an organization called Athletes Helping Athletes. In addition to its anti–drunk driving program, AHA delivered the Student-Athlete Leadership Program, which trained high school athletes to serve as mentors in elementary schools. I discovered immediately that as much as I enjoyed talking about important issues, I was more interested in empowering young people to find their voice and use their personal stories to address the issues facing their community. I worked with AHA for nearly twenty years, training high school athletes to conduct classroom workshops with elementary school students. Working with AHA was one of the most important experiences of my life. Connecting to the next generation extended beyond imparting the wisdom of my experiences. It was also about passing the baton to younger athletes who delivered messages on civility, caring, and successfully navigating through life. The work never felt like a "job." I was leveraging my position as an athlete in a manner that brought congruence and purpose to my life. It was always a joy, until the day I was forced to question the very foundation on which my credibility stood.

DISTORTED IDOLATRY

One of the most gratifying things I did with AHA was to bring high school students to the elementary schools they had attended, where they would give presentations. One day I found myself involved in an awkward exchange with a group of fifth-grade boys. Normally I would merely supervise the high school students, allowing them to do the work; however, this particular classroom became unruly and I had to step in.

A few minutes into the session, I could see that the high school students were struggling. A small group of fifth-grade boys were disrupting the class. As I entered the room, one of the high school boys, feeling relieved, introduced me to the class and mentioned I was a professional football player. The class—the boys in particular—erupted.

"Who do you play for?"

"What kind of car do you drive?"

"How much money do you make?"

I answered none of their questions and attempted to settle the room so the high school students could finish their lesson. The boys were relentless, so I allowed one question. "How much money do you make?" one asked. Artfully, I declined to answer. They responded by offering figures for me to confirm, starting at ten million dollars and gradually descending from there. Once they reached four million, they gave up in disappointed disgust, proclaiming that I was not really a professional football player.

I was focused in that moment on the class as a whole and ensuring that the high school students got through the rest of their lesson. But the vociferous response from the boys stirred up a burgeoning angst and dissonance I was feeling about my high-profile status. The superficiality of celebrity was compromising the depths and complexity of being a competitive athlete.

I thought back to when I was ten years old and the New York Giants player Gary Jeter was the guest speaker at my youth football awards dinner. I remember being in a state of debilitating awe because an NFL player was at the local catering hall. The innocence and wonder I felt so many years earlier had been replaced by these fifth-graders' cynicism, the pursuit of athletic excellence reduced to a quest for material gain. This felt antithetical to what sports should be about for kids. The same thing that gave me credibility distorted my identity and my values in their eyes. They saw the business, not the game; they saw the privilege, but not the work it took to achieve success. It made me question what they valued about my presence and what they respected.

I was sad because, on some level, I understood their response. I was a caricature whose identity was not only reduced by the expectations others had for me as an athlete, but who was beholden to the source of my privilege—the business of professional football. It was undeniable, and at the time I had to accept how the hyperbole of sports was central to the reason I was even in their classroom in the first place. This hyperbole is the hype with which sports are interpreted and sold by the business: the extreme winner-take-all, do-or-die presentation of sports that portrays athletes as superhuman warriors who pursue victory at all costs.

I simply wanted to use my platform as an athlete to reach young people on important social issues. Yet that platform was bolstered by a kind of privilege that had become an obstacle to my mission in their classroom. Almost every one of their assumptions was anathema to the lessons I was trying to teach. Money, cars, and fame were by-products of a more selfish and destructive interpretation of success in professional sports, one that was disrespectful, uncompromising, and grossly disregarded the "other," no matter who that may be. That was neither who I was nor what I wanted them to understand. However, my identity had become a myth and inextricable from my privilege. I couldn't deny one without denying the other.

My privilege spoke for me, no matter what I felt or how I tried to diminish or deny its influence over my life. And, like most athletes, I never wanted to take the uniform off. But my work with young people made me realize that I was no longer riding *with* the wave of my privilege; I was riding *against* it. I began to wonder if that had been the case all along. Was my privilege a burden? How wide was the chasm between how I saw myself and how others saw me? And what myths had I unknowingly perpetuated and advanced in my ignorance?

I know many athletes will fully recognize and understand this dilemma. Similarly, musicians, actors, and others whose identities have been morphed by their talent, fame, or money struggle with remaining grounded and uncorrupted by the trappings of their newfound privilege. In many ways we are similar to those born into social or economic privilege who do not recognize it because it's all they have known.

I experienced this dilemma most of my life and actively worked against what people thought and expected, no matter if that perception was positive or negative. It was a constant and desperate attempt to maintain an identity separate from the perceived advantages others assigned to me. Privilege is typically evident in what one has in relation to others, and more clearly visible to those who don't have it. Those who have power and privilege often only see the ways they lack both. As a professional athlete I was driven by the insecurity of not being the best, a feeling that lingered even on the day I entered the College Football Hall of Fame and wondered why I belonged. The uniform that gave me angst about my worth also made me work harder to keep it and allowed me to maintain the assumption that I was functioning in a meritocracy. It was misleading and disingenuous to believe that the primary factor in my success was my hard work. In truth, it was my God-given talent, for which I could not claim responsibility.

As I approached my final years of playing football, I often thought about those fifth-grade boys and their distorted understanding of sports and success. Retirement would certainly provide more time to focus on those issues and hone my skills in delivering more effective messages to them and other young people; however, the thought of shedding my football uniform—in both a literal and metaphorical sense—also meant ridding myself of the identity that gave me credibility with them. I feared that once I discarded that identity, they would no longer respect me, and my ability to have a meaningful impact would be diminished.

In the end, I retired on my own terms in 1994. I found a passion for something that burned as strong as my desire to play the game, and retirement helped me find focus and direction. But it was not without that moment all athletes dread—being told that your value and skills have diminished. As I will explore in the next chapter, that moment also exposed the greatest blind spot of my identity as an athlete and a man.

RICHARD LAPCHICK

The transition period from football to my new life lasted about seven hours. That was the time it took me on a November afternoon in 1994 to drive from Lansdowne Park in Ottawa, Ontario, where I played my last season of football, to Northeastern University in Boston. I cleaned out my locker, hit the road, and arrived in time for a two p.m. staff meeting at the Center for the Study of Sport in Society.

Earlier that year, Warren Breining and I had visited the Center and its founder Richard Lapchick. Richard is a global leader in sports activism and one of the world's foremost voices on "racism and sports." He is also son of Joe Lapchick, one of the first head coaches of the New York Knicks and a member of the NBA Hall of Fame. Joe played in the NBA when it was an all-white league. In 1950, as coach and executive of the Knicks, he signed Nat Clifton, one of the first black players to play in the NBA. Following the move, Joe Lapchick went from legend to pariah. He was jeered, harassed, and received death threats. Young Richard watched as "fans" threatened the "nigger lover" he called Dad.

This inspired Richard to devote his life to using the platform of sports to confront racism. He put his life on the line, literally, as a leading voice during the movement against apartheid in South Africa. Like his father, he faced threats to his life and displays of hate, though even more intense and deliberate. One gruesome episode happened in 1978, when he was leading the movement to ban South Africa from international sporting events. Following a protest of the Davis Cup tennis tournament, he returned to his office on the campus of Virginia Wesleyan University and was met by two men who beat him and carved *Niger* (they failed to correctly spell the intended slur) in his chest with a pair of scissors. Richard, undeterred, relentlessly continued his work against racism. In 1994, he received a personal invitation from Nelson Mandela to attend his inauguration as president of South Africa, a testament to the unique and influential power of Richard's voice.

Just a few months after that inauguration, I joined Richard's staff at the Center. I was eager to work with him and particularly to observe him—a white man using his privilege to confront racism in sport and society. I admired him for making the *choice* to use his privilege and social position in a unique way—to confront other white people of power and privilege and encourage them to acknowledge, understand, and eradicate the racism that their privilege otherwise allows them to ignore. His goal and approach is never to criticize, demean, or shame his peers, but to provide the opportunity for them to live up to the best of their humanity. And for those who deserve harsh rebuke, Rich's gentle demeanor still possesses a sharp edge that is uncompromising and unequivocal.

Although confronting racism was not at the center of my work, race was the core of my life experience. Aside from my athletic ability, my race shaped my life and experience as a football player. I was not just a quarterback, but a "black quarterback." My success put me in proximity to a privileged class that has offered me invaluable advantages over the course of my life. Yet, despite the tangible ways football enabled me to transcend many forms of racism, my position as quarterback was met with great resistance by a sports culture and larger society unprepared to cede significant or even symbolic leadership positions to black people, reminding me of the ways in which I was not privileged. Still, I was part of the legacy of black athletes like Nat Clifton who were living beacons of the larger fight for social justice. I appreciated that I stood on the shoulders of the black athletes who came before me, opening the door for the opportunity and privilege I enjoyed. It also made me conscious of my responsibility to do likewise for the next generation of athletes.

Watching Rich use his privilege to voice the need for social justice opened my eyes to the essential work white people must do. Rich ventures deeper than an abstract, ideological stance against racism: he takes on the cultures in which racism is systemic yet unacknowledged. Through his disarming demeanor, he gets to the heart of the matter by looking past one's malicious intent, presenting the facts not to criticize but to provide opportunities for action. Throughout the years that I worked with

Rich and watched him engage white men of power in sports, politics, and education, I realized that his impact is uniquely transformative.

Rich doesn't simply proclaim that he is "okay" with or tolerates black people; instead, his work says, *I am a white man purposefully using my privilege and am willing to sacrifice it for truth and justice.* The people he most affects are white and may not have the eloquence or even the courage to verbally recognize their white privilege, but their hearts, and perhaps their consciences, are relieved just by associating with him. He gives them the opportunity to demonstrate the best of themselves.

As a black man, I am grateful for people like Richard Lapchick. It is an unavoidable truth that he could easily have chosen not to jeopardize his privilege, especially when the violent forces of racism literally threatened his life. As his friend, I am indebted to his honest and forthright humanity.

When I joined the staff at Northeastern University to work alongside Rich, I arrived at a time and in a place for which I thought my entire life had prepared me, as if I had reached the middle act of a perfectly scripted film. Although the move to Boston was a bit disorienting, as it was the first city or town I had lived in since the age of fifteen that I did not associate with the game of football, I felt a tremendous sense of purpose being there. As a former athlete with a unique story of my own regarding racism, which I told through the context of my sports experience, I embodied the core mission of Rich's work and the Center. Success in football enabled me a privileged platform from which I intended to address myriad social issues—including racism.

That all changed when I met Jackson Katz, and the script of my life and its purpose took a dramatic shift, like what you would find in a Quentin Tarantino film. And though the same characters and story line remained intact, a new point of view was established, one so distinct from the original that it *felt* like a different story altogether.

JACKSON KATZ

Jackson Katz cocreated the Mentors in Violence Prevention (MVP) project in 1993, a year prior to my arrival in Boston. MVP, one of several social justice programs founded at the Center, is a gender violence prevention program, designed to engage male college athletes and fraternity men to confront gender-based violence on college campuses. Violence prevention was a new issue to me and, specifically, gender violence—in terms of sexual assault and domestic violence—was as foreign to me as the concept of gender itself. My initial inclination was an old one: the platform of sport was so powerful and universal that it could shoulder any social justice issue, and if it could help effect change in apartheid South Africa, then surely it could help protect the victims of violence. But Jackson and MVP were not simply focused on *protecting* potential victims of violence or even confronting perpetrators. While much of the programming was structured to provide strategies to achieve those goals, the broader objective was real culture change at the foundation level, interrupting the social paradigms that nurture and perpetuate violence and reinforce its role in our society.

MVP was the program that introduced the "bystander" approach to the work of preventing sexual and domestic violence. Unlike the way bystander "intervention" is more generally used today, MVP intended to engage men like me, who did not see or understand the problem. Teaching men to acknowledge and confront the ubiquitous culture of patriarchy and sexism in which we live was the brilliance of MVP's bystander approach.

Racism (in sports and society in general) was a big issue

and I understood it from my lived experience. It was *my* issue. I knew my athletic success gave me a particular privilege not afforded to many black men or athletes, one through which I could address the issue in a broad, comprehensive, and powerful way. However, after spending more time with Jackson and learning about the goals and content of MVP, I realized he was asking me to access *a privilege I did not know I had, to confront an issue I never realized was mine.*

I learned the undeniable truth about violence in our society, which is that it is overwhelmingly perpetrated by boys and men. What is more, the multiple forms of violence committed against girls and women (including sexual assault, rape, harassment, and domestic violence) are nearly exclusively committed by boys and men, and most often by men with whom they are intimately familiar. Yet the violence committed against girls and women is defined by *their* experience, *their* inability to avoid the violence or whatever causes it. We first assign blame to them for "provoking" or pissing off the "wrong guy," then create systems to deal with *her* trauma, but not *his* behavior.

The use of violence in relationships is most often not the result of a male being "provoked" into an unusual and sudden fury, but a pattern of manipulative and calculated power and control through the threat and use of violence. What was new for me was understanding the issue of men's violence against women as *my* issue. As an educator drawing on my experiences and working with young people on a range of social issues, why did I never understand or see this as my issue, or recognize my role in addressing it? How had my lack of awareness affected my relationships with women? And how did my ignorance perpetuate the general silence on this issue?

In many ways, my ignorance can be attributed to the patriarchal forces that position men's violence against women as "women's issues." It is analogous to how I had framed the issue of racism: my valid position to talk about racism drew its legitimacy not from my perspective as a privileged athlete but as a victim in a valued segment of society—sports. In this regard, just as with men's violence against women, the victim becomes the focal point from which we consider the issue. This is a function of power and is one way in which it is insidiously maintained—if we only analyze these issues from the victim's perspective, then we fail to examine the power that shields perpetrators from examination.

BYRON HURT

When I began working with Richard and Jackson, I immediately understood that I was in the company of a different class of men: those who examine their own privilege with honesty and depth and are unafraid to risk that privilege to expose and confront hard truths. I admired them both tremendously. Their leadership and courage were compelling and I was immediately inspired. Then I met Byron Hurt, the assistant director of the MVP program, and I saw that he was a social justice pioneer like Richard and Jackson. But we shared a deeper commonality—we are both black and former college quarterbacks.

As I discussed race and gender with Byron, I began to realize that *my life had been more adversely affected by my gender than by my race*. I fought constantly against forces that, knowingly or unwittingly, sought to keep me "in my place" because of my race; however, being unaware of the more dogmatic and ubiquitous influence of patriarchy, I was a lemming when it came to understanding the overall impact of gender.

When Byron and I first met, he told me how, when he was growing up on Long Island, he wanted to go to Syracuse University and be the next "Donnie Mac" (my nickname). I was flattered and simultaneously had a familiar feeling of validation—the privilege afforded me as an athlete. But it became quickly evident that we bore similar scars from our experiences as black quarterbacks. We laughed and shared our stories and travails—facing blatant racism by coaches, teammates, and fans who did not want to accept a black quarterback. The conversation organically turned to masculinity and how it was the buttress that enabled us to hold our heads high through the toughest periods of our journey.

Byron and I were among a growing number of black quarterbacks who wanted to be viewed as not just athletes but as intelligent, thinking leaders who were respected and who admirably represented our schools and communities. Talking with Byron was like every exchange I had with the black quarterbacks who came before me. Doug Williams was the Super Bowl MVP my senior year of college, and during my NFL career I was a backup to both Randall Cunningham and Warren Moon. At that time in the late 1980s, the three of them were the only black quarterbacks starting in the NFL. Though from the outside it may have appeared that our experiences were different, we were bonded by the reality of being black men in one of the most coveted positions in sports.

But with Byron, the conversation changed in a way I did not recognize, and he did something I did not expect: he gave language to what I had not previously considered. He spoke about power, privilege, and race, and linked them to masculinity—that part of my identity I had not examined in my life. Our bond was not simply as black quarterbacks but as *men* who grappled with the compromises asked of us by the culture we so desperately wanted to be a part of.

Although I was officially a colleague working alongside Jackson and Byron, I was also a student, learning from them in a way I had not anticipated. Initially, I was just an observer of their work as they conducted workshops and seminars, honestly and forthrightly examining masculinity and the links to men's violence against women. It was powerful to watch them work with a team of male athletes and get them to open up about social dynamics that were otherwise very difficult to discuss. The emotional demands of the discussion seemed impossible, yet the urge to participate was irresistible; I was fascinated by the challenge of engaging men in this uncharted conversation and was personally compelled to explore my own place in it.

BELLY OF THE BEAST

In early 1996, Rich Lapchick, Jackson, Byron, and I were invited by the University of Nebraska's legendary football coach Tom Osborne to conduct a series of educational meetings with his team. The invitation followed two disturbing cases of assault committed by Nebraska football players Christian Peter and Lawrence Phillips. Peter, a defensive lineman, was cited for several violent incidents, including sexual assault, dating back to his freshman year in 1991. Phillips, who at one time was a front-runner for the Heisman Trophy, was charged for the vicious assault of an ex-girlfriend. At the time it was the most high-profile case of men's violence against women in the sports world, largely because it involved one of the most successful programs in the history of college football.

As our plane touched down in Lincoln, I remember saying to my colleagues, "We've just landed in the belly of the beast."

Byron was sympathetic to the fact that, for virtually all of the players on the team, this was the first time they would discuss the violence committed by their teammates. Moreover, he reminded me that this would be the first time any of them considered the culture of masculinity as part of that violence.

When we walked into the football facility, I felt at home. I knew several of the team's coaches, and the photos on the walls included former Nebraska players I had played with and against during my pro career. Down one hall, the year-by-year results lined the walls and I stopped at *1984*, the year Nebraska came to Syracuse as the number one team in the nation and we beat them 17–9. This sense of familiarity also made me realize how much I had learned and grown in the two short years since I retired from the game.

I was a highly competitive athlete for twenty years of my life. It was a life characterized by relentless focus and strict discipline with single-minded purpose. Walking through Nebraska's facility, I actually identified more with that creed than with the ideology of a social justice educator. I was acutely aware of what we were asking the team of men to do—to put that athletic mind-set "on pause" and engage in a discussion about a culture of masculinity that is often enmeshed with the expectations of them as football players, and to examine that culture's link to *their* violence against women. And it was the very same culture that had afforded me the privilege to ignore my full identity.

THE ROOTS OF MY PRIVILEGE

My new insights about masculinity helped explain why the experience I had with those fifth-grade boys was so significant at the time. Having occurred shortly before I retired from football, it forced me to reevaluate my identity as a football player and the role that identity played in my work with young people. They were just immature boys, misbehaving and acting as if they knew everything about sports. Their behavior earned the tired old saying, "Boys will be boys." The teacher excused their behavior because they were "so excited" to see a professional athlete in their class. Yet their disruptive behavior was the reason I had to step into the room in the first place. Their rudeness warranted a firm response; however, the teacher's decision to not correct them but make excuses for them instead was rooted in the general belief that their disrespectful behavior was inevitable. They simply lacked the discipline and self-control demonstrated by their classmates.

It's also important to note that not all the boys in the class exhibited this behavior. It's revealing that we allowed *some* of the boys to disrupt the entire class with impunity. Both the teacher and I dismissed their behavior as a function of being male. This is condescending and sexist—and all too common.

The expression "Boys will be boys" is typically used when boys' behavior ranges from less than desirable to outright deplorable. It's most often invoked as an excuse for grossly inappropriate or dangerous behavior and sometimes delivered with nostalgia for a simplistic form of masculinity devoid of the maturity and personal responsibility of "manhood." This is the most dangerous blind spot of masculinity because it neglects the roots of violence and violent behavior.

When Jackson challenged me to access a privilege I did not know I had, to confront an issue I never realized was mine, he named the forces of patriarchy, sexism, and misogyny behind that privilege. He helped me recognize how I participated both actively and passively in sexist behavior in the form of jokes or bravado. He also helped me see how a culture of sports that enforces an unyielding and rigid gender identity necessarily ignores the damage done not only to women but also to men.

Jackson was not simply casting stones but illustrating how these social forces are part of the structural foundations of men's violence against women and the collective silence about it. While the issue of violence was easy for me to identify, I had more trouble understanding my privilege because it was invisible in my daily life. To do this required more than reflection and introspection; I had to incessantly examine those things around me that I was never challenged or required to consider or deal with *because* I was a man. And although I am a black man, and my blackness means I have less privilege than a white man, I cannot ignore the advantages of being a man in a culture where patriarchy is the principal architect of the social order— its religious dogma, business principles, and the hierarchical structures of virtually every institution, from family to govern- ment. The role of patriarchy to shield masculinity from scrutiny is ubiquitous and invisible, but when masculinity is exposed in the gender binary and isolated in the context of men's violence against women, we are faced with a disturbing reality about men, as well as with society's virtual silence on the topic.

In light of the statistics regarding violence committed against women, it is staggering how permissive our society is about a culture that nurtures, perpetrates, and supports that vi- olence. Every incident of men's violence against women, regard- less of what form it takes, reminds us of the urgent imperative to examine masculinity. But for me, as a man, they are also re- minders of a distinct privilege. Women experience certain daily realities regarding their personal safety that rarely, if ever, enter my consciousness as a man. This paradigm goes unrecognized yet is as present as the air we breathe—it is part of male privilege and rendered invisible by the assumption of its normalcy. While our silence about that privilege may be an act of *omission* rather than *commission*, it nonetheless constitutes an abuse of privi- lege. Our silence as men weaponizes our privilege; it is abuse by silence and omission that enables so many overt acts of violence.

THE PRIVILEGE OF CHOICE

The extent of my privilege as a man was not simply confined to that afforded me through sports or the lack of scrutiny of my masculine identity. While football supported my advancement on a path I chose, my masculinity allowed me a privileged position and *choice* to engage in the work to end men's violence against women. During my early years in the work, it was not uncommon to be one of very few men in a room of professional colleagues. This made me more aware of the greater world that remained less engaged and indifferent to the issue.

On an absolutely beautiful day in late May 1999, I attended a luncheon at the famed Tavern on the Green on the west side of New York City's Central Park. The luncheon was a celebration of women and their work in support of women's rights and opportunities. The reception prior to the award ceremony was held outside. Small groups of women and men gathered beneath the budding trees or sought out the sun to enjoy its warmth for the first time that year. Outside the confines of the restaurant grounds, the park was brimming with activity. New Yorkers were taking advantage of the endless recreational opportunities the park offered to shed city living: horseback riding, paddleboats, games on the softball fields, and enjoying the Great Lawn, which has hosted major concerts and even a visit from the pope. Central Park in spring is spectacular.

Inside the restaurant, the atmosphere was festive and the conversations were full of empowerment and optimism. I found myself huddled with a group of friends from the Lifetime television network. As we reviewed the program and the illustrious list of honorees, one of the women in the group commented how much she admired a particular honoree. But she also just wished "she wasn't so . . ." She caught herself as her words trailed off.

I could not let it go and pressed her: "So . . . what?"

Sheepishly, she replied, "So angry."

She knew referring to the "angry feminist" was particularly offensive. The rest of the group let it go. But I could not. Immediately I commented on the perfect weather and gorgeous setting of Central Park, arguably the most amazing urban park in the world. Tavern on the Green is at 67th Street and Central Park West, an affluent Manhattan neighborhood. The east side is not too dissimilar, as property along the park is prime real estate. I asked my friend if later that evening she would feel comfortable leaving the restaurant, putting her headphones on, and going for a jog back to her apartment on the east side of the city. Sharply and in a matter-of-fact tone, she responded, "No, I'm not crazy!"

It was hard to imagine that one of the greatest urban parks in the world, in one of the greatest cities in the world, bustling with healthy activity, was also considered unsafe for women just a few hours after that luncheon. I quickly pointed out that there was a time when it was unsafe for me, as a black man, to cross the park alone. That changed, in part, because of the work of white people who confronted the violent racism that led to the lynching of black men who were "not where they belonged." I then referred to the alleged "angry feminist" and said, "She has every right to be pissed off about that disturbing reality." Her anger was justified and her activism to change that reality was what we honored that afternoon. Like other honorees that day, she was courageous and unapologetically fierce in her work to secure women's safety in a world indifferent to that cause.

Several years later I attended a similar event, the one with Vice President Biden and I as honorees. We were honored for the same work, at an event held in the same city, where conditions of women's safety had hardly changed. Yet no one considered us "angry." *We* were allies—good guys! Our motivation was neither criticized nor questioned; instead, we were lauded for raising our voices. We both made the *choice* to fiercely and unapologetically stand with women as allies. That choice is part of our privilege. We could very easily have chosen not to, and blended into a patriarchal society of ubiquitous male privilege that few men notice. Our voices may have been augmented by political position or athleticism, but this dynamic was fundamentally rooted in our identity as men.

It would thus be disingenuous to not acknowledge the privilege of our gender. In a field rightly dominated by women, our presence was no different than Richard Lapchick standing in solidarity with Nelson Mandela and Muhammad Ali for the global cause of racial justice. Race should not matter, but it does. For Joe and me, our gender should not matter, but it does. And for me, being a football player should not matter, but it does.

Working as an ally in solidarity with women to address men's violence against women, while critically important, often feels like a bare-minimum effort. Recognizing and using my privilege is important, but without a true and honest interrogation of that privilege, I would be incapable of being an ally of men as well, as they confront the issue and explore their personal growth. Though my privilege has given me the position and platform to be an ally, I have had to honestly examine the origin of my privilege and how it functions, and to do so independent of my position as an ally to women.

When I retired from football, I feared I would be stripped of the privileges the game afforded me. But retirement gave me clarity on the source of my privilege. I was twenty-nine years old and thought I was walking away from the most important influence in my life. But the "end" was actually the beginning of a profound awakening.

 *Twenty-Nine*

WHO AM I WITHOUT THE GAME?

At the end of the 1993 Canadian Football League season, nine months before I went to work at Northeastern University with Richard Lapchick, I decided to retire from football. After eighteen years of playing the game, I felt the time had come to walk away and I was determined to control the inevitable. In the months that followed, I parted from my seasonal nomadic lifestyle, confined myself to one residence, and turned full attention to one career. For the first time since elementary school, I had to consider a daily schedule that did not involve a purposeful physical workout. I was adjusting nicely, back on Long Island and doing work I loved.

I truly believed I was done with the game, then I received a phone call from Adam Rita, the new head coach of the Ottawa Rough Riders (now the Redblacks). Fifteen minutes into our thirty-minute call, in my head I was already back in a familiar routine: planning the next day's workout. The following morning, I was in the gym preparing for season number nineteen.

A few months later, I arrived at training camp in Saint-Jean, Quebec, a small town an hour south of Montreal. But it was quickly evident that I had overstayed my welcome in pro football. One of the most difficult things for an athlete to do is retire from their sport on his or her own terms. Most athletes have to be told that it's time to retire by a coach or organization; or they realize themselves their heart is no longer in it; or, worse, their bodies succumb to time or injury, forcing a reluctant surrender. My career essentially ended through a combination of all three factors. My mind was elsewhere, and my heart was no longer committed to the work necessary to prepare my body to play. I lacked the enthusiasm I once had for the game. I thought I could "fake it" and survive on talent and experience.

In many ways, I was the same player I had been earlier in my career. But as training camp progressed, my waning desire to prepare became evident even to those with whom I was playing for the first time. For those who knew my career, it was obvious. Unfortunately, those people were Coach Rita, the team's general manager, and the owner. Each of them had expectations of me far greater than the production I showed in training camp. After camp ended and the team returned to Ottawa, I was summoned to a meeting. Every football player dreads that moment you're told to attend a meeting with team management and to "bring your playbook." The playbook is the only thing you have left that they still want. It was a foreboding sign of imminent dismissal from the team.

However, this meeting was different—not as fatal as I anticipated. To ease my anxiety, they immediately told me that they did not want to cut me from the team. But they could not justify my contracted salary as the number-three quarterback on the roster. They offered me the league minimum salary to stay with the team. After considering their offer for a brief moment, I began to cry.

I was well aware of why I was crying, and it was not the demotion or dramatic reduction in salary or the end of my career. In fact, it would have been a relief if they'd cut me and sent me home to get on with my life—for that I was prepared. Instead, the tears expressed an irony that cut deeper than I was willing to examine. Despite my great love for football, I never wanted the game to define who I was as a person; yet, for all the opportunities and privileges it provided, I realized in that moment how limiting that privilege had been to my life as a whole. At that moment, I was forced to recognize and understand the person I was without the game of football.

Most athletes have three names they go by: their given name, used by family and close friends; their media name, used by fans; and the name their teammates call them that signifies camaraderie, affection, and style. I have always been "Donald" to my family, "Don McPherson" to the public, and "Donnie Mac" to those guys who were my brothers in the game. Donnie Mac still wanted to hear his name called by teammates, for it was that fellowship that made football the game I loved. So I accepted the league minimum salary and remained with the team.

I spent most of my time that season in earnest reflection on my relationship with the game and, more specifically, the business element of sports that changed the game I played in my youth. In the early 1990s, media were advancing the business of sports in a way that made the game unrecognizable to me. In other words, I rationalized that it was not me but the commercial focus that dimmed my passion for the game. I wasn't ready to consider my frailty and vulnerability. That I was no longer physically capable or mentally focused or tough was an inner truth I was no more capable of understanding than I was prepared to confront. Those were questions for the feckless and weak to face when they failed. As a successful athlete, I was an archetype—a consummate model of the powerful and privileged athlete. However, I was forced to face the inevitable questions: Was I ready for a life without football? What would happen to "Donnie Mac" when I left the game, and would

"Don McPherson" be equally as interesting and effective in the classroom talking to young people without the mantle of "athlete"?

At the time, I didn't see how the privilege afforded me by my success as an athlete was a blind spot to understanding myself as a whole person and man. Although I never took my talent or the opportunities for granted (I was deliberately and intentionally working to leverage my football career for a professional life after the game), I also had never prepared for the chapter of my life when my physical identity could longer mask my emotional, psychological, and intellectual identity. I cried that day in Ottawa because I had allowed myself to be duped by that privilege and the culture in which it was nurtured. At that moment in time, both were unquestioned and unexamined.

If you asked me what it was like to play in the CFL, I would have spoken from the perspective of an American living in Canada and a former NFL player. Both "American" and "NFL" cultures served as the comparative lens with which I held personal attitudes and expectations about living in Canada and playing in the CFL, respectively. If you asked me what it meant to be a football player, I would have pridefully lamented the hard work, discipline, and accountability to team that defines the culture of the game, something that friends and fans never witness. If you asked about being a quarterback, I would have given a painfully nuanced account of the noble loneliness of leadership and strict attention to detail. If you asked me what it meant to be a black man, you would hear me identify with my generation. Born at height of the civil rights movement of the 1960s, I witnessed and internalized the ways that my generation understood and confronted the assemblage of violent racism throughout society.

I was, and remain, fully aware of the indelible influence these cultures had on me. I wore them like the football jersey that represented the school or city for which I played, or the color of my skin that could not be shed when the game ended. They were my psychological and emotional appendages, unique parts of me I used to navigate my daily life with explicit intent and purpose. However, if you asked me what it meant to be a man, that description would have been less complex and would've lacked a sense of ownership. So much of being a man, I thought, was something you just did; there wasn't much to *feel* or *think* about. But that was about to change in the next stage of my life.

A few weeks into that final season in Ottawa in 1994, Richard Lapchick phoned and asked if I'd be interested in a position at the Center. When he called, I was in a restaurant with a few teammates. I excused myself and took the call in my car. It was raining heavily as I sat in a dark parking lot in an unfamiliar section of Ottawa. The setting was completely foreign and the moment was equally strange: I was accepting a (real) job offer that would alter my life as profoundly as the game of football had.

Once back in the restaurant, I immediately informed my teammates that I was moving to Boston to work with Richard Lapchick. They could see my excitement as well as my realization that my desire to play football had never been there in Ottawa. In a phone call, I had done what many athletes never achieve: I transitioned out of the game on my own terms and with a passion for what came next. Although I was thrilled, my decision initially conjured more fear and insecurity than the day I tearfully accepted the league minimum salary to stay with the team.

BOSTON

For many athletes, transition is a way of life; adjusting to new teammates, coaches, and cities is a constant and often as unpredictable as opening the sports section of a newspaper to the "transactions" column to learn of players who have joined or been released from a team. Athletes themselves can learn of their departure in exactly that manner—the harsh reality of the business is literally in "black-and-white."

By the time I reached professional sports, transition was as routine as off-season workouts. As a freshman in high school, I decided to transfer to another school that had a more successful football program. Every subsequent move to another city was, likewise, made for the sole reason of advancing my football career. The game dictated every move, and my identity and social status as a football player preceded me. I attended Syracuse University on a scholarship to play college football, joined NFL teams in Philadelphia and Houston, and lived in two Canadian cities, Hamilton and Ottawa, to play for the CFL. Boston was the first city I would live where I was not playing football, something I had been doing since the age of ten.

Initially, it felt routine; the privileged and charmed life of an athlete provided me a soft place to land. I was working in an organization that valued my sports background and professional aspirations; I was hired as codirector of a national AmeriCorps program at the Center called Athletes in Service to America. I joined the sports radio team at WBZ, the number one radio station in Boston, covering NFL games. My arrogance led me to believe it was business as usual. Then one day I received a call from Fran Charles, a local television sports news anchor. He had heard me on the air and learned that I was working at Northeastern University. He wanted to do a "Where are they now?" segment for the evening news. As I hung up the phone, I remember thinking it was odd because I never played football in Boston, so why would anyone care? I was a "has-been," a trivia question for sports junkies. Still, there was a veneer of confidence I had developed over the years that portrayed something more like cockiness and bravado. As a retired athlete, I thought, it was better to be a "has-been" than a "never-was." I did the interview and was suddenly back in the spotlight as an athlete. Although my days as an athlete were behind me, it still had a social currency that I was happy to embrace.

In the professional world, however, I *was* a "never-was," a neophyte. It was like I was fresh out of college in my first real job. But I was twenty-nine years old. Working on a college campus, I felt even less adequate; professionally, in a field flush with academic achievements and degrees, my primary credential was work experience as a professional athlete. While I felt welcome among the learned professors, researchers, and administrators, it was clear I was an intellectual lightweight and not a member of the academic elite. Though I had worked on social issues for several years, in the greater professional community in Boston, I quickly realized I was, in many respects, an anomaly.

Despite a litany of insecurities and daily life adjustments, I didn't give up the social habits of the privileged life I had led as a young professional athlete. It was not long until I discovered Grille 23 & Bar, which was walking distance from my office on campus. Grille 23 remains my favorite restaurant in Boston and is the quintessential steak house with servers in lab coats, white linen tablecloths, and a menu of hefty steaks, Scotch, and cigars (smoking was permissible and encouraged). It reeked of cigars and privileged masculinity. It was decidedly *not* the typical hangout of the new employee earning an entry-level salary from a local university.

One evening after work, I sat at the bar to have a cigar and a glass of Scotch. Sitting next to me was a man several years my senior, enjoying the same exorbitant vices. He was charming and intelligent, with silver hair and impeccable style. After a few exchanges regarding the cigar maker and Scotch vintage, he asked what I did for a living. Knowing there were very few, if any, patrons in Grille 23 who spent the day considering how to deliver dating violence prevention programs to middle school students, I felt a rush of insecurity. I crafted my response accordingly: "I am codirector of a federally funded initiative to mobilize college students to address men's violence against women, racism, and academic success, housed at Northeastern University's Center for the Study of Sport in Society." He nodded with an unexpected and knowing look of approval. He worked in the health care field and acutely understood some of the challenges of the work I described. He continued with several questions, most of which centered on my personal path to that particular field, which was quite unusual at the time. When he asked questions about my ideological and pedagogical approach, I gave answers that were sufficient but lacked depth. He was observant and quickly realized that my pursuit was not an intellectual one founded on extensive research or policy analysis. Showing sincere interest, he asked what I did before coming to Boston. Sheepishly, I revealed that I spent the previous seven years working with community-based programs in schools in New York and . . . playing professional football. The look on his face went from curiosity to bewilderment.

In 1995, there were relatively few men actively engaged in the work to prevent men's violence against women. There were even fewer (well, none, actually) who had retired from professional football to do so. Three decades later, I get the same look and the same questions. Did something happen in my life? To me or someone I loved? Was I a perpetrator?

I never minded the questions—in fact I understood. Primarily because I did not fully understand myself. It felt like a natural progression in my work, using the platform of sports to address important social issues. But now I no longer had football as a platform, and I began to ask the same questions of myself. Why was I passionate about the work? Why had I chosen *this* field to leverage my experience as a professional athlete?

LOOKING BACK FOR GROWTH

I wish I could say my transition from football was completed within that seven-hour window between cleaning out my locker at Lansdowne Stadium in Ottawa and attending my first staff meeting at Northeastern University. But it was not that simple or linear. My transition took place during a period of immeasurable change and growth. It didn't unfold as I expected, as a carefully charted course for the future; instead, it was an honest and detailed interrogation of my past.

I was no longer the gladiator whose armor told the mythical story of a warrior-athlete. Nor was I an experienced professional with a résumé of accomplishments to support the confident and self-assured demeanor with which I approached my work. I recognized immediately that I had to understand the source of my confident demeanor if I was to fully understand the work I was about to take on. So I began reflecting on and learning about my privileged masculinity, including how I learned it and how it served as the greatest influence of my life.

In one respect the transition felt easy because, although I was not 100 percent focused on the game, I was certain about why I was done. I had spent my final season of football examining how the business of sports was changing the game I played in my youth. Primarily, I had observed the change in the attitude and behavior of young players who, responding to the evolving commercialism of sports, seemed less interested in the history, tradition, and love of the game and more focused on their place in the business. This experience soured me and left me grasping to find altruism and "transferable skills" in the game that applied in the real world and had redeemable social value. Ironically, the more the sports media tried to make the next generation of athletes seem more accessible, the more distant they became, with every interaction solidifying a relationship between them and the public that was almost entirely commercial in nature. In many ways, as I've stated, as football players we become less human and more like caricatures of masculinity—tough, strong, unemotional warriors who are locked into the zero-sum proposition of sports ("I win, you lose"). Yet, now that I was retired, I could see how this perspective is valued by the greater culture, even though it doesn't mesh with life at home or in the workplace.

I thought again of the fifth-grade boys I had encountered, the ones who cared more about my salary than my athletic skills and experiences. If their interpretation of sports and who I was as an athlete did not align with what I valued or intended to deliver, what other messages were being conveyed that I was unaware of? Despite my insistence to the contrary, how much of my identity did they have right? After all, I had returned that final season to keep "Donnie Mac," a character in my head, alive. In order to be effective in talking to boys, did I have to confront the very culture that gave me identity and privilege? And was I prepared to do that?

LINEAGE OF LIES

The more time I spent with Jackson, Byron, and the MVP program, the more I began to see how I had been duped, how narrow my understanding was of masculinity, and how significantly it shaped my identity. I not only questioned my former perspective but considered the men in my life who blindly adhered to the same perspective—my father, uncles, brothers, coaches, and teachers who had all been raised by and passed down the same set of narrow, dogmatic rules about what it means to be a man. I should say that while none of those relationships were perfect, I would characterize them all as loving, trusting, and caring. However, in every given moment the men demonstrated and enforced the rules of masculinity and its specific behaviors, often in uncomfortable, threatening, or violent ways.

I began to see masculinity as a set of mandated behaviors that are part of a *performance* for the approval of other men. Like most men, I never questioned the narrow rules—doing so would be antithetical to obedient and disciplined masculinity. As an athlete, acute discipline served me well; being unemotional and tough, ignoring one's pain and that of others, remain hallmarks of highly competitive sports. But the same rules of masculinity applied to men who were not competitive athletes. This is partly why I became a caricature: I had to serve the vicarious experience of fans who viewed me and so many male athletes as representative figures of masculinity.

During this journey of reflection and introspection, I often wondered, *How did I get this far in life without fully considering or understanding masculinity?* As a leader of fellow athletes and an educator of young people on important social issues, how did I miss this critical analysis and perspective? More profound was my realization about the "why": the culture of masculinity made me blind to *why* I never recognized or felt compelled to confront it. I was a man in a man's world. *It was as if my masculinity was this invisible force working on my behalf and for my benefit, yet without my permission.*

The invisible force is patriarchy!

The more I learned and understood how the narrow rules of masculinity are learned and maintained, the more clearly I saw those moments in my life when my wholeness was suppressed.

Looking back, I often feel like Malcolm Crowe, Bruce Willis's character in the 1999 film *The Sixth Sense*, in which he dies and becomes a ghost in the opening scene, though that fact is concealed from the audience until the film's conclusion. He remains invisible to all except a boy with the gift to see dead people. Audiences were stunned to finally learn that Crowe was a ghost for the entire film. The illusion works because it is rooted in the assumption that he, like all men, is emotionally impotent. An evasive communicator, emotionally tormented and work-obsessed, Crowe the ghost is not too dissimilar from living men.

Reflecting on my life revealed a series of emotionally incompetent moments that lived deep in my memory. They told a greater story I needed to examine. These moments were not traumatic, but they did fully display my emotional incompetence, even though I felt wholly empowered as a man.

VULNERABLE WARRIORS

In 1988, when I was a rookie in the NFL with the Philadelphia Eagles, we traveled to London to play a preseason game. During the week prior to the game, we were offered an assortment of opportunities to experience and enjoy London. Keith Jackson, the great tight end from the University of Oklahoma, was the first player picked in my draft class with the Eagles and my roommate during training camp and on road trips. He was one of the most gifted athletes I've ever known and a man of strong faith and a generous heart. Keith and I were the only two on the team who chose to attend the world's longest running musical at the time, *Les Misérables*, at the Palace Theatre. I don't think either of us had any idea what the play was about—just that it was a unique thing to do in London and was as far a departure from football as possible. It was a fairly sophisticated activity for a pair of twenty-two-year-old NFL players to choose.

There is a powerful moment in the play when the main character, Jean Valjean, is visited by the ghost of Fantine, who died earlier in the play and returns to escort Valjean to heaven. When Fantine died, Valjean pledged to care for her daughter as his own, and now Fantine has returned as he is about to die. It is a poignant and highly emotional moment. As I felt the tears welling in my eyes, my thoughts immediately turned to Keith, concerned that he would see me crying. I leaned back in my seat and looked at the ceiling, believing perhaps that gravity would force the tears back. I wrenched my neck to see if Keith noticed, only to see him with his head down and pressing his thumbs between his eyes, looking for the button that makes tears dry up. The scene we were watching was an extraordinary display of human redemption through faith and obedience to God and love for others. It was a perfectly legitimate moment to be human and respond emotionally. But we visibly struggled to show our emotions as it violated an ingrained rule of being a man that had been reinforced all our lives.

One of the primary rules of being a man is that one must respond to emotionally charged moments with steely indifference. Crying is never allowed. This is one of the great ironies of masculinity: it takes courage and toughness to live authentic and emotionally competent lives; shutting down or hiding from our truth and wholeness is more of an act of cowardice than it is of courage. Granted, there are a few special exemptions—if Keith and I were to shed tears of joy for winning a championship or of despair for losing one, our emotion would be acceptable. However, in the context of showing empathy, vulnerability, compassion, or love, our tears were stifled, our emotions muted and ignored. We chose to attend *Les Misérables* out of authentic curiosity and interest, but sitting in the Palace Theatre that evening, we chose to be guarded and less authentically whole.

I remember that moment vividly, as I remember so many other times in my life that I ignored and suppressed the wholeness of my humanity for the "performance of masculinity." The performance never felt authentic—that is the very essence of a performance. It is about following a script, a set of rules and expectations provided in advance that govern how we as boys and men behave and interact with each other, thus creating the "culture of masculinity."

For many years, I never considered how profound that moment in the theater with Keith was. If I ever told the story to others, it was because it was funny. But while the story of a couple of NFL players fighting back tears at a musical may sound like the setup of a joke, the inability of many men to recognize and understand their feelings and live as emotional beings is a troubling reality that can lead them down a lonely, painful, and often tragic path.

Several months after our trip to London, I went out with a few friends to a nightclub. It was a quiet night and I decided to go home early. When I got in my car, I received a phone call with the news that a college teammate, Wes Dove, had fatally shot himself. Most people who knew Wes would quickly describe him as a "gentle giant." He was six foot seven, muscular, and as kind and unassuming as a man of his size could be. He was also quite intelligent. The news was paralyzing. I could not drive, and sat in stunned silence trying to grasp the fact that he had killed himself in such a violent manner. It made no sense and left me in a place of confusion, sadness, pain, and anger.

I eventually composed myself enough to drive and did so aimlessly before stopping at a diner where I sat over a cup of coffee and searched for meaning. I was despondent, staring into space between measured outbursts of emotion. I was also rather conspicuous, still dressed for the nightclub in a half-empty diner, crying over a cup of coffee. A police officer took the stool next to me. He asked if everything was okay, certain that I was drunk, high, or coming off some traumatic altercation. He was looking for physical evidence of my trouble while I was searching for an understanding of Wes's emotional pain and torment.

I told him about Wes, and we talked. I had a million questions, and since he was the first person I was able to unload on, he heard them all. "Why didn't he call? Reach out? What could have been so bad? When does it get that bad . . . ?"

The officer was professional and polite. He listened to my interminable line of questions but soon grew impatient. "Your buddy would want you to be strong," he said. "Have a cup of coffee and get home safe." Although he remained professional, his tone reminded me of my father asking me why I was crying and telling me that he'd give me "something to cry about" if I didn't pull it together. It was a jolt that made me cognizant of my surroundings. Quickly, I pulled myself together and left the diner. I drove home feeling embarrassed about my emotional display yet numb to everything else—incapable of understanding Wes's pain and reluctant to process my own.

Today, if you mention the suicide of an NFL player, chronic traumatic encephalopathy (CTE), the degenerative brain disease caused by repeated head trauma, is immediately blamed as the culprit. The physical damage done to the brain is easy to comprehend and, in fact, makes sense given the barrage of collisions that football players experience. But since Wes's death in 1989, I have lost more than thirty-two former teammates and fellow players. They weren't merely people I knew through playing the game—they were personal friends. None of them lived to age fifty. Whether their deaths were self-inflicted or caused by some other ailment or life decision, they were all warriors—men who disregarded their physical and emotional well-being to play a game that required they push harder, feel less, and ignore all that distracted them from the pursuit of the game, including themselves. In the end, they were made vulnerable by the very thing that made them warriors . . . and I was no different.

THE REAL IMPACT OF SPORTS

Athletes are routinely praised for the ability to "tough it out," to fight through pain and ignore our vulnerability and fears. But we are no different than most men, who are conditioned to function without using their full emotional repertoire because they lack the emotional intelligence and practical experience to use feelings as essential tools for navigating life. If men display this emotional repertoire, the response from other men is swift and decisive: they view it as a form of betrayal to the power that has been passed on to them by previous generations of men who nurtured them in the performance of masculinity.

At twenty-nine, I began to see how well I had mastered the performance. I accepted the self-inflicted emotional scars and wounds because they were medals of honor that showed I had survived some imaginary battle against weakness or vulnerability. Yet the people who awarded me those medals only valued me as a warrior who performed for their entertainment—at the expense of my full identity as a whole person. I had not survived. Rather, I had delayed the inevitable—that moment every man faces, when he realizes he didn't say "I love you" enough or put away his pride more and hug those he cared about, living in *unashamed and vulnerable wholeness*.

Admittedly, when I retired from football and moved to Boston, I was not in search of my "unashamed and vulnerable wholeness." Part of me was pursuing a career that would allow me to fulfill what I believed to be my purpose in life, to use the platform of sports to serve others. I believed the rhetoric that proclaimed the altruistic mission of sports: to inspire leaders and build character and integrity. But upon gaining some distance from my experience, I took a more sober and honest look at the evolving role of sports in American culture from every angle (youth sports, parenting, race and gender, media, business, and so on). My analysis, as well as my need to utilize sports as a tool for social good, all led me to a troubling place. As I drilled deeper toward the root cause of each social problem, it became increasingly difficult to glean positive lessons from the culture of sports.

This is not to diminish the tremendous and profound ways that sports impact lives and communities. But as the business of sports evolved and changed the ways in which sports function in our society, it has also become antithetical to many values sports once purported to advance, so much so that I began to wonder if those values ever existed in the first place. I was compelled to honestly examine the true impact of sports on society, especially on young people. I had to answer, with painful veracity, an essential question of whether sports are good for children. Beyond the clear benefits—the feelings of nostalgia, moments of charity, and pride in one's community—what were the neglected priorities of our sports-obsessed culture? What was the impact of the hyperbolic way in which sports are portrayed? What misleading messages were young people—boys, in particular—receiving that were detrimental to their development as whole people?

I THOUGHT IT MATTERED

In the waning years of my career, I sought to answer some of those questions as I grew more focused on my work outside the game. Initially, the ways in which sports were changing upset me as an athlete, and only became more troubling as I reflected on my role as an educator. The distorted perspectives of the "fifth-grade boys" revealed a value system perpetuated by the business of sports that has eroded the fundamental qualities of sports in our cultural understanding. The "show" of sports and pursuit of exorbitant revenues has supplanted and usurped process and preparation as foundational qualities of participation.

I struggled with this reality in my first few months after retirement. I felt let down by the game, not because of a lack of personal success, but because of how little it actually prepared me for life after the game—one of the fundamental altruistic assumptions was the transferable skills acquired through sports participation. My parents raised me to be independent of their care; my teachers prepared me for life after school; and all the adults in my life, including coaches, attempted to impart life-long lessons. However, in the end, I realized that as an athlete I was engaged in a self-centered pursuit that I was led to think mattered more than it did. That old familiar paradigm—"I win, you lose"—applied in an intensely competitive game in which the shelf life of a player is very short. The business peddles such hyperbole not to nurture the altruism but to exploit it. The aggregate lessons of my sports experience left me empty, searching elsewhere for compassion, integrity, and a sense of community.

A few months after I retired from football, I began to write an unwieldy manuscript titled *I Thought It Mattered*. I became obsessed with the business of sports—the thing I believed had robbed me of my passion for it. The book was based on my accumulated experience as a player and as an advocate attempting to harness its social virtues. Its title came from sober conclusions I had arrived at after a process of examining the true impact of sports in my life and the ways its social function had changed. That process revealed what I knew intuitively but had not fully examined—that the aim of sports had never been as noble and altruistic as it was presented to me and widely understood as a social asset. Ironically, I am the beneficiary of the period of sports when, the more the business grew, the more ineffective the game became in delivering on its supposedly altruistic mission.

I wrote *I Thought It Mattered* over a three-year period that was a cathartic process in which I named, detailed, and liberated myself from my blind loyalty to the strict doctrine of sports. This was not easy or without personal angst as I enjoyed many aspects of the culture in which I was raised and later thrived. I understood how that doctrine served an effective role in my life as an athlete. But as a man, I had to extract myself from it to grasp its impact on the core of my whole identity.

Thinking back on that fateful day in the team office in Ottawa when my football career essentially ended, I remember feeling like a "sucker." I returned for that "one last season" thinking I would find something meaningful: perhaps a sense of closure on a relationship that had consumed two-thirds of my life. I was searching for the payoff that was supposed to come from all that loyalty, commitment, and sacrifice. The things referred to in the inspirational quotes that rang in our heads as athletes, which, in the end, were just used to sell an idea. We constantly heard phrases such as, "Winning isn't everything, it's the *only* thing," and, "Leave it all on the field," but there was nothing in this rhetoric to prepare me for when it was over. And while one of my favorites, "There is no 'I' in team," is certainly true, what happens when the "team" is no longer there? Who am "I" without the team?

At twenty-nine, I retired from the one thing I thought mattered most. It brought so much privilege to my life that it also made me reluctant to see it as privilege, and to see the flaws that my success had excused. I was forced to acknowledge the extent to which the privileges of masculinity had shaped my identity. As I began to navigate life without that privilege, I saw my masculinity for the first time. And I came to understand the tears of a seven-year veteran of professional football—a grown man as vulnerable and scared to step off the field as an eight-year-old stepping onto it for the first time.

THE ASSUMPTION OF ALTRUISM

At the time I was writing *I Thought It Mattered*, I was committed to the utility of sports as a tool for social impact. After all, if we didn't believe that assumption, why else would we, as a culture, think sports could help eradicate so many ills and social problems such as racism, drug addiction, breast cancer, obesity, and a litany of others?

At the Center for the Study of Sport in Society, I became part of the culture that expected sport to shoulder that burden without honestly and intentionally recognizing the ways in which sport itself needed to be interrogated, confronted, and held to account for its adverse impact on society. The notion that sports can "fix" social issues, or that its platform is so powerful that it can adequately carry a message of social change, is rooted in the assumption of altruism attributed to sports and supported by the arrogance of sports culture. One of the greatest assumptions about sports is that it is inherently interested in progress and social justice.

Sports historians and "stewards of the game" will wax nostalgic about groundbreaking sports icons like Jesse Owens, Althea Gibson, Jackie Robinson, and Billie Jean King—pioneers whose courage and skills were "allowed" to be displayed. However, when athletes authentically express views that challenge societal conventions and the business interests of sports, the response is less generous. In 1968, Muhammad Ali was stripped of the heavyweight boxing title and jailed for his antiwar position, a position based on his Muslim faith. When Ali died in 2016, he was lionized and praised as the "greatest of all time"—the label he gave himself. But the nostalgia for Ali was revisionist history: sportswriters and other journalists were perpetuating a myth. Ali did not just refuse to serve in the military; he brashly explained to "white America" why he refused, famously stating, "I ain't got no quarrel with them Viet Cong," and, "No Viet Cong ever called me nigger." This statement and position, taken at the risk of incarceration, makes Colin Kaepernick's decision to kneel during the national anthem seem like a minor expression of one's First Amendment right to free speech. However, Kaepernick's actions, taken the same year that Ali died and was widely celebrated, have exposed a hypocrisy about the way sports co-opts social issues to advance its bottom line. For example, the NFL proudly supports breast cancer awareness, cobranding the NFL shield and displaying pink ribbons. It's a worthy initiative but is largely targeted toward a consumer population the league wants to grow—women. Despite its public relations problems with domestic and sexual violence, the league has had a more tepid approach to publicly address this issue. It is easy and safe to appeal to women's need for cancer-screening awareness and not so simple to address the issue of violence against women, without being accountable for the culture of masculinity that is perpetuated by the business of sports and the overwhelming population of men who consume their products.

Kaepernick's protest not only revealed a deep racial division that seems no less healed in the fifty-plus years since Ali faced prison for refusing military service; it also exposed the manipulative tactics sports executives use to thwart social movements and campaigns.

Athletes like Ali who broke racial and gender barriers were

not viewed as social justice activists but rather as individuals who demonstrated an indomitable spirit and courage once they were permitted the "opportunity" to withstand people's hatred. Their humanity and identity as citizens were not valued, only their athleticism and talent. That was the real commodity and the only part of their identity that was valued.

Sports were never intended to inspire social change or to work for social good. We assign those attributes to the (primarily) male athletes we admire, and we admire them for how they perform as athletes, not who they are as people. We have placed sports and athletes so high upon a pedestal that we have long ignored or excused the behavior of those whose actions away from the game are antithetical to the ideals we attribute to sports—leadership, integrity, respect, and community.

SELF-SCOUTING

My critique of sports, no matter how harsh, is not meant to diminish the countless amazing "feel-good" stories or outreach programs that serve kids living on the margins of society. I would argue that sports are where inspiration and learning happen *not* because they are innately good, but because they provide a platform and opportunity for caring adults to be genuine catalysts for change. Indeed, sports can be inspiring, but the assumption that they are inherently a positive influence is not just wrong but counterintuitive.

Every great athlete and team "scouts" their opponent through what is known as a "SWOT analysis"—a rigorous inventory of the adversary's strengths, weaknesses, opportunities, and threats. Athletes also apply that level of analysis to themselves so they may identify and perfect their strengths, but also, more importantly, recognize their vulnerabilities and weaknesses. This is called "self-scouting."

At twenty-nine, I completed a thorough self-scouting process, noting how the culture of sports socialized me as a man. The process helped me identify and focus on those things about sports that I truly love and that have made me a better advocate and educator. Twenty-nine was also the age at which I first considered masculinity as the most powerful and significant influence in my life. It may have been happenstance that this process began only after I left football; however, I do not believe one step would have occurred without the other.

Masculinity needs a stage upon which a script, based on a set of expectations, can be performed. The performance is done for the approval of a patriarchal society that wrote that script and assigned virtue to the narrow qualities of masculinity. Every man knows his stage: the family, job, or peer group where he is required to perform and prove he is a "real man." But he also recognizes the stage for what it is, knowing it is not where he can be a whole man. Ultimately, I was fortunate that my stage was football, where the performance of masculinity was visibly exaggerated. Peering through the prism of a successful athletic career, I could more easily do the work of deconstructing the myths of both sports and masculinity.

Hyperbole and Myth

MY WORST PERFORMANCE
WAS MY GREATEST MOMENT

My worst performance as a college football player was the greatest moment of my life as an athlete.

It was the final game of the 1987 regular season against West Virginia University (WVU). Prior to the game, we accepted an invitation to play in the Sugar Bowl, scheduled several weeks later on New Year's Day. The Sugar Bowl was a major accomplishment, but completing an undefeated season is the ultimate goal of every football team. The last (and only other) undefeated Syracuse team was the 1959 national championship squad that played in the Cotton Bowl. For WVU, a victory would earn them a bowl game of their own, so the stakes were high for both teams.

It's hard to imagine today, but even with so much at stake, the Saturday-evening game was not nationally televised. But when WVU scored to take the lead with just ninety seconds left in the game, ESPN and a national television audience tuned in, expecting to witness an upset. What they saw instead was one of the most dramatic finishes of any game in Syracuse history. I led our team down the field and, with ten seconds left on the clock, threw a touchdown pass to our tight end, Pat Kelly. We were an extra point away from tying the game with only a few seconds remaining. There was no overtime in college football in 1987, so our choice was to either kick an extra point and tie the game or run a play to earn two points and the win.

Without hesitation, we decided to go for the win, risking suffering our first and only loss of the season. We executed an option play perfectly and tailback Michael Owens squeaked into the end zone. We won, 32–31. There is not a more dramatic and emotional way to end a perfect season. None of us had ever experienced a win, or season, like that one. We immediately knew the significance as the fans stormed the field. Our place in Syracuse history rested on more than just having an undefeated record—we had become one of the best teams in school history and I was called "the Man."

Those final moments, however, did not reveal the truth of my performance. I had played the worst game of my entire football career since I started playing at age ten. But because the bulk of the game was not televised nationally, most college football fans only saw my last-minute heroics. Faithful fans in Syracuse who may have attended the game or listened on the radio barely remember how awfully I played that evening. Most only *want* to remember the last moments that were marked by the cool-under-pressure way we pulled off the victory, seemingly unfazed by the intensity of the situation. The first fifty-nine minutes (of a sixty-minute game) were forgotten, leaving me to be lionized for the last sixty seconds of play.

When I think of that game, I fixate on my mistakes. In spite of what others saw or think they saw, for me the memory holds feelings of insecurity, vulnerability, and fear of failure. I had spent my entire life to that point using football and sports as a mask, to hide and suppress those feelings. It served me on *and* off the field, as I learned that the qualities for which I was valued as an athlete were also linked with what was expected of me away from the game: to remain cool, never showing emotions. The game of football provided an ideal stage to nurture and demonstrate the outward expression of no expression at all.

THE PROCESS OF SPORTS

There is an important distinction to note about sports' ability to mask and suppress feelings—it is destructive and ultimately counterproductive. I could not rid myself of the emotions or the frailty of my humanity, but I could learn to identify and harness those parts of myself through what I call the "process of sports." Gaining mastery of a sport is a process of practice and preparation through which an athlete replaces insecurity and fear with the confidence and competency that come from astute study, the repetitive application of sound principles, and support from the people around them.

However, the "process" of sports ignores a key paradox: being vulnerable is human; embracing our inherent fears and insecurities and excelling in spite of them is the height of the human experience. This is primarily why sports are so compelling for athletes and spectators alike. Sports offer a communal experience in which players and fans do not have to embrace their human vulnerabilities and shortcomings—they can vanquish them. We quickly and unequivocally assign those "weaker" qualities to our opponents in the zero-sum "us vs. them" paradigm of sports. This hyperbolic interpretation is essential to fans' and players' sense of their superiority.

While hyperbole is how sports are sold to spectators, the process of sports is where true love of the game is found. This applies not just to sports but to any endeavor. Those who excel in anything requiring mastery of a skill or discipline—whether in science, the arts, medicine, or trade—fall in love with process, with practice and preparation. That is the reality of sports: to compete is to have the opportunity to demonstrate what you have learned and meticulously prepared for. You don't get better on game day, you get better preparing for game day. What made my worst performance also my greatest moment was that despite my dreadful play for virtually the entire game, my preparation mitigated the impact of my mistakes and ultimately defined the moment. What had been taught and instilled in me over years as an athlete, and in that particular game plan, took over in the "heat of the moment"—the decisive instant when process and preparation are manifested as instinctual behavior. I often think the realization of this dynamic conclusively answers the philosophical "nature vs. nurture" question: one must possess the ability or inclination, but training and preparation inform the execution. It applies to human behavior in general: we are socialized to behave a certain way in the heat of the moment, in a way that only appears to be instinctual, but it is more often a conditioned reaction.

But these ideas about process were not in the fans' minds when they stormed the field at the culmination of my college football career. They did not see the extensive nurturing of my talent, the long years that entailed pain, frustration, and many failures; instead, they only saw what to them was my natural talent shining at the right moment. And because they didn't see that long process of preparation, they didn't see the real me, "Donald." They were fans of the exaggerated role I fulfilled in performing for them, which let them vicariously identify as the "winner" of the game. The community hailed me as a local sports hero and role model for children. Likewise, for my teammates, I was a leader and winner. They saw only what served and upheld the image they needed me to represent.

MONETIZING THE HYPERBOLE AND MYTH

I was called "the Man" not because of who I was as a person, but *what* I represented: the embodiment of a hyperbolic sports narrative and a heroic performance in the heat of the moment. However, my true self lived and loved the process; I was never in the hyperbole of a moment, though it consumed those around me—fans, friends, and even family. I remained attuned to my insecurity and the angst I felt about it, because I knew therein lay the drive to sustain my focus on the rigors of the process. As my career advanced, the chasm widened as more people saw only the caricature I had become, a tool of the sports business and a symbol of the school and community I represented. And, unknowingly, the myth of masculinity incarnate.

"The Man" is a myth, a fictitious character that depicts an unrealistic yet romanticized version of masculinity. He demonstrates and promotes behaviors that uphold the notion of what a "real man" is *supposed* to be: tough, strong, unemotional, and impervious to pain. He is also successful despite being defined by such limited qualities. But because he is narrowly defined, he needs an adversary—someone or something to overcome or conquer and a stage upon which to perform. Football was my stage.

Football is a uniquely American game. Its roots are in working-class, rural Pennsylvania, and despite its crude beginnings, it has seminal links to two important arenas that shape and define American masculinity: the military and higher education. After all, two of the founding fathers of the National Football Foundation were General Douglas MacArthur and longtime Army football coach Earl "Red" Blaik (the other was journalist Grantland Rice). Each year, when the NFF gathers in New York City to induct a new class of college football Hall of Famers, it's a veritable tale of American masculinity in service to country and the hallowed game of football, played on behalf of academic institutions.

These links help bolster the proud identity of colleges and communities of all sizes, which respond by placing a disproportionate level of importance on the game. While football sits atop the hierarchy of sports, other sports also assume a high social position. Coming of age in the 1980s, I lived and played through the era when the business of sports seized upon and exploited sports' widespread appeal for commercial interests where generating revenue became paramount.

Subsequently, this has changed the way all sports function in our society, especially in our schools and communities, because *all* elements of sports are now monetized. The competitive event is the most prized commodity. It surpasses in importance the outcome of a win or a loss and the training and preparation that preceded it. Success is measured in terms of attendance, viewers, or clicks. The athletes, their teams, and their venues merely serve as the "big tent" for a multitude of products and services to be sold.

Schools, communities, and fans monetize the vicarious identity and pride they feel as supporters of winning teams. The sports business exploits the hopes and dreams of those communities, hyping the clash of rival fan bases and perpetuating a grossly false narrative where only the event matters. At the center of all of this are athletes, intensely and obsessively engaged in the mundane details of the process. They are expendable widgets in a business that only values those who advance its bottom line. The irony of their position in the business is that they are at their competitive best when they approach their sport with the youthful optimism that comes through *play*, the only thing that is truly free.

THE BUSINESS OF SPORTS KILLED PLAY

For many children, sports are innocent play and a fundamental way in which they begin to intimately understand the world around them. Play is central to their daily activity and development. As they grow, sports can be a powerful socializing tool, but how and what they manifest largely depends on the adults in their lives. If adults believe in the myth and hyperbole of sports, the impact can be destructive. What's more, the business of sports to which children are incessantly exposed is not interested in creating new athletes, but instead new consumers of the myth and hyperbole. Ultimately, it seeks to expand consumption and the numbers of fans, TV "package" subscribers, video game users, fantasy league customers, and ticket holders. At every level, the business leverages the emotional connection we have with sports—the joy, purity of play, and our youthful aspirations.

In the 1990s, as sports in general were splintering from their supposedly altruistic roots, people were greatly concerned that the culture of youth sports was deteriorating as well. One of the most alarming indicators was the behavior of parents in youth sports. This led me and my colleagues to conduct countless workshops and hold discussions with leagues and parents in an attempt to "keep sports in perspective." In one workshop, a mother asked how to deal with being told her son was "not good enough to play" and how to communicate that message to him. When I asked the son's age, she replied that he was eight. I was immediately disgusted with whoever made that assessment of an eight-year-old, wondering how that coach could not understand the concept of play. There is actually no such thing as not being good enough to play. However, the real blame lies with the sports culture, as well as with an industry of elite travel leagues and specialized coaches, for co-opting the play of children to serve their economic agenda. His play was not good enough to serve the burgeoning business of youth sports (elite travel leagues, specialized coaching, etc.). When I was told that I was not good enough at the age of twenty-nine, it was communicated in terms of my financial worth, which hurt to hear at that age, so I cannot imagine what it does to a boy to hear he's not good enough, when play is so integral to his existence.

Whether it's an eight-year-old boy or a twenty-nine-year-old pro football veteran, one's physical ability does not negate one's desire to play. This is how the business of sports can have such a negative impact, especially for many boys. In the beginning, their relationship with sports is pure and innocent, yet as they get older, the opportunities to engage in play wane. They keep that desire to preserve that pure relationship, which the business of sports exploits for profit. Meanwhile, the identities of those boys remain connected to narrowly defined qualities associated with sports.

Sports are the ideal platform to perpetuate the myth of masculinity. Male athletes are caricatures of narrowly defined masculinity. Their performance is viewed as the quintessential demonstration of toughness, power, and strength displayed in the meritocracy of competition. Patriarchy has long appropriated those rigid qualities as "manly" and sports provide a stage upon which they can be performed. The resulting paradigm is one in which the hyperbole of sports is used to perpetuate the myth of masculinity.

PULLING BACK THE CURTAIN

Every corner of power and influence in American life is governed by patriarchal values that work to maintain male privilege. These values are full of contradictions, consistently revealing blind spots of privilege and an unsettling hypocrisy in the lives of many men. The contradictions are most crudely evident in the myth and hyperbole of sports. We profess selflessness yet remain obedient to a dogma that is self-serving; we claim integrity in our leadership yet obfuscate and mask our true selves when we are challenged; and we profess toughness and courage as fundamentals of masculine identity but are cowards when we are faced with the hard truths about our humanity.

I do not wish to make a blanket indictment of sports; however, when leaders in this field are challenged on issues of integrity, often their response, paired with subsequent damaging revelations, is painfully incongruent with the values they profess to uphold. As I demonstrate in the three accounts that follow, this hypocrisy can be toxic in situations where boys are responsible for harmful behaviors and horrific crimes. And the hypocrisy can be damaging to all involved, whether perpetrator, victim, or bystander.

Our Guys: The Glen Ridge Rape and the Secret Life of the Perfect Suburb, a book by Bernard Lefkowitz, was published in 1997. It is a penetrating examination of a community reluctant to acknowledge the violent, predatory behavior of a group of a town's high school athletes. The boys, primarily members of the Glen Ridge, New Jersey, high school football team, gang-raped a high school girl with cognitive disabilities on March 1, 1989. The girl was lured to the basement of a home in this affluent suburb by the promise of a date with a player she liked. Her disability made her more vulnerable, and it is precisely that which the boys preyed upon. In objective terms, this was a perverted and sinister crime. However, as Lefkowitz emphasizes in his book, this horrific ordeal was defined most profoundly not by the boys' crime but by the response of the community that came to the defense of "their guys." During the criminal trial that lasted nearly six months, a disturbing reality slowly emerged: the predatory violence of male athletes was being rationalized, defended, and normalized.

Twenty-three years after the Glen Ridge crime, members of the Steubenville, Ohio, football team raped an intoxicated, unconscious girl. This time, it was videotaped . . . by the boys themselves. During a session of extremely heavy drinking, the victim passed out. Her seemingly lifeless body became a tool for high school boys to demonstrate their inhumanity and validate their dangerous notions of masculinity.

Both victims were considered to have a limited understanding of the crime as it occurred: the girl in Glen Ridge was living with cognitive disabilities; the girl in Steubenville lost consciousness. In both cases, our attempts to understand the heinous crimes committed by boys with no prior records or history of violence were further confounded by the community's vehement defense of them. From a distance, it seems preposterous, but it is very commonplace because the members of a community's football team are stars, the embodiment of town pride. Denial is a typical response: "Our family/community could not produce such depravity and evilness." "Nothing like that happens in our community."

In these situations, one of the first defensive strategies people take is to blame the victim—this deflects attention from themselves and their community. *She* must bear some form of responsibility simply for being present and making herself vulnerable to the "innocent" yet uncontrollable sexual urges of "good boys." Or: she succumbed to a greedy desire to associate with power and privilege. This is particularly a defense when high-profile men are involved. It does not matter if he is "America's Dad/Comedian," a Hollywood mogul, a trusted newsman, a Supreme Court nominee, a professional athlete worth millions, or even one of several local high school boys ordained as stars of the community. This is the most grotesque form of victim blaming, and it has been the standard approach to discrediting and silencing women's voices on men's violence, harassment, and discrimination. Again, all of it is legitimized by the myth of "the Man" and the narrow ways in which successful masculinity is defined.

The rush to defend boys in cases like those in Glen Ridge and Steubenville keeps us from examining and holding to account their foundational attitudes and the expectations they have for themselves and their peers. We must go further and examine the impact of our blind adoration of a sports culture that promotes a disturbing concept of masculinity. One unchecked and very problematic assumption is that it is part of men's essential nature to commit violence against women, that it is a central element of masculinity. But when we press deeper, we find the violence is not confined to, nor does it emanate from, that original intent. The propensity for violence is internalized in boys through their socialization. Author and activist Bell Hooks explains how this process works:

> The first act of violence that patriarchy demands of males is not violence toward women. Instead patriarchy demands of all males that they engage in acts of psychic self-mutilation, that they kill off the emotional parts of themselves. If an individual is not successful in emotionally crippling himself, he can count on patriarchal men to enact rituals of power that will assault his self-esteem.

MEPHAM

A stark illustration of the process Hooks describes is found in another horrific case of sexual assault. In the late summer of 2003, three high school students were raped repeatedly over the course of several days while away at a camp. The attacks were brutal and incomprehensible: the perpetrators used a broomstick, golf balls, and pine cones to penetrate their victims; to intensify the pain, they applied "heat-producing" mineral ice to each object. The assaults were so violent and severe that one of the victims required surgery for the sustained injuries. Several bystanders reported nothing to camp authorities even though they witnessed each assault taking place day and night *for three days*.

Imagine a child you know—a high school student in his or her first year, eager to explore new opportunities—being ambushed by these attacks. Or picture that same child as a bystander, witnessing this barbarity and being helpless to do anything about it, knowing it was going to happen again. Does it matter if the victims are male or female? Does it matter if they know their attackers and the bystanders?

It should not matter, but in this case it does. To truly understand the depths of how the hyperbole of sport advances and perpetuates the myth of masculinity and what Hooks calls "the rituals of power that assault self-esteem," these details matter. In this case, the identities of the victims, perpetrators, and bystanders matter in helping us to understand why and how this crime took place. They also reveal how our distorted reverence for sports can lead to our values being compromised.

The victims were ninth-grade boys, and the perpetrators and bystanders were their teammates on a high school football team. Yes, members of the same *team*. The Wellington C. Mepham High School football team had traveled from Bellmore, New York, to the hills of northeast Pennsylvania to facilitate a single-minded focus on football. Training camp was meant to isolate them from their hometown and its presumably negative distractions. This is a common practice in the sport on all levels. Along with eliminating distractions, it expedites unity and cohesion among the team members. The goal is to accelerate bonding and form a brotherhood to buttress the group against all the opponents it will face in the upcoming season.

Tragically, the unanimity created did not help this team win games. Instead, it imposed a shroud of silence over both victims and bystanders of this heinous crime. The silence was sustained when the team returned home. It was not until more than a week later, when one of the victims, who required anal surgery, revealed to his mother that he'd been repeatedly assaulted by his "teammates."

Once exposed, the entire incident became known as a "hazing scandal," suggesting it merely involved the mishandling of an unsanctioned yet purposeful common practice. Hazing became the problem and the threat the team needed to target. The public discussion turned to logistical concerns such as appropriate athlete-to-coach ratios at camp and the proper way to supervise players in their cabins. The actual crime of sexual assault was ignored, and a bizarre alternative was inserted into the discourse that allowed the community to avoid conducting a difficult and complex examination of the attacks. Some members of the community even castigated the victims for speaking out, blaming *them* for the subsequent cancellation of all games that season. The entire town became starkly divided, as many vocal members of the community believed *they*, the victims, had betrayed the "brotherhood" of the football team.

At the time of the Mepham case, I had been retired from football for seven years. I tried to comprehend what happened at this camp. When I was a young player, we euphemistically called training camp "torture": it was a stressful, hypercompetitive, and draining experience that challenged the physical and emotional limits of each individual and the team as a whole. I could not conceive of the physical and psychological burden of being raped between practice sessions.

I was forced to recall the hazing I witnessed and experienced as a player. Though I always fully disagreed with any kind of hazing, I understood the process and did the silly things I was told to do to "entertain" the veterans and demonstrate humility. I carried water buckets, was taped to a goal post, and was booed as I stood on a chair in the cafeteria and sang my alma mater. None of it made me feel any more part of a team. In fact, it was counterproductive, as I lost respect for the guys who reveled in the behavior, even though I understood the need for levity, even when it came at the expense of the newest members of the team.

By all measures, Mepham is a model school—part of the accomplished Bellmore-Merrick Central High School District. But neither the school nor the community was prepared to address the disturbing realities this crime exposed. For example, the public discourse never examined why the perpetrators chose rape as a tool to foster solidarity. Why had none of the bystanders felt compelled to share what they had witnessed to their coaches, parents, or *anyone* (save for confiding to a few classmates, which led to rumors in the school's hallways)? What kind of trauma did the bystanders experience as spectators to their friends and teammates being raped?

Despite all the attempts to avoid the painful truth by not using the term, rape is what occurred. Forced penetration, without consent, was used as a means to "welcome" boys to a team. The tactic was deliberately chosen to coerce submission and to humiliate and dehumanize. The impact of this unspoken truth remains in the hearts and minds of every boy present at that camp. And because public consensus determined this was a hazing incident and nothing more, we failed to confront the psychosocial havoc it undoubtedly wreaked in their lives.

Generally speaking, one of the primary distinctions that sets hazing apart from other crimes is the essential role of bystanders. With most crimes, perpetrators prefer silence from victims and to avoid witnesses altogether. However, with hazing, the victim requires proof that he or she endured the pain and humiliation and survived it. It is necessary to gain credibility and that is only achieved through the presence of bystanders; their role is to bear witness and validate the abuse.

The pivotal role of bystanders is too often forgotten in our analysis of hazing. When we attempt a simplistic interpretation of a case like the Mepham crime, we fail to consider bystanders' trauma because we view them as co-conspirators. We neglect the emotional and psychological trauma of those who have to rationalize and compartmentalize what they've witnessed. The moment the Mepham attacks first occurred, they had to reconcile the barbarity in front of them with their own notions of civility, humanity, empathy, caring, and masculinity. And they had to remain relatively unfazed—any reaction, especially if expressed from a position of empathy, would invite unwelcome attention. The bystanders also had to internalize their own suffering and rationalize their inaction to protect their friends during each subsequent assault.

While the coaches at Mepham High School maintained they had no knowledge of the sexual assaults, they did know that some sort of hazing was underfoot. As investigators documented after the 2003 incident, the football program's history with hazing included well-known traditions such as "Freshman Friday," when freshman suffered a multitude of humiliations the day before a game. To be clear, Mepham is not an outlier. Many coaches, across all sports, expect their veteran players to "show younger players the ropes" in order to further player development, maintain discipline, and focus on team goals. Typically, the veteran players are given leeway to use strategies overtly or tacitly approved by their coaches.

To hold the coaches accountable for the sexual assault seems arbitrary. However, they had a unique influence, and the culture and climate they created governed how they expected the boys to behave.

The violent sexual nature of the attacks demanded questions and answers from all of us. Parents had to come to terms with the fact that their sons had witnessed these horrific rapes and said nothing. Coaches either did not recognize or chose to ignore the physical and emotional trauma that was occurring each day of training camp. Once they learned about the attacks, they had to reconcile with their encouragement of the hazing, even if they didn't realize the extent of the violence. Bystanders had to find the intellectual and emotional means to compartmentalize what they had witnessed and, by their silence, participated in. Within our communities, we all must consider the culture that shapes the mind-set of "our boys"—how it can produce terrible violence and enforce a silence about it.

SILENCE SUSTAINS VIOLENCE

James "Whitey" Bulger was one of this country's most notorious organized crime bosses who led Boston's Winter Hill gang for decades. Bulger was one of the most prolific and violent criminals in US history, committing several murders and engaging in racketeering, drug dealing, and extortion. During the trial that sent him to prison for "life" for his crimes, what he denied most vehemently was that he was a "snitch," supplying information to law enforcement on the crimes his cohorts committed. Nothing could be worse for a career criminal than to be labeled as someone who discloses the truth about the crimes he witnessed or conspired to commit. It makes me think about the Mepham bystanders and so many other groups of boys who maintain silence about the violence and abuse they witness and inflict upon each other. In many ways, they had the same moral code as Bulger. They accepted the brutality because they feared being labeled a snitch. Fear of retribution is not the only motivation to be silent. Privilege and the protection it provides also serve as subtle yet powerful levers.

Being the son of a New York City internal affairs detective, I grew up familiar with the code of silence in the organized crime community. My father respected the decisive, unapologetic way that criminals applied the code. It was part of their cold toughness that he admired. Similarly, he appreciated those in sports, particularly coaches, who functioned in a blunt and abrupt manner. It was an aspect of football he enjoyed most—the tough, win-at-all-cost approach. He, like all the coaches throughout my life, was from a generation that valued a harsh, uncompromising form of nurturing that is affectionately called "old school."

My father was hardworking, tough, and stoic—an old-school dad. He may not have always agreed with the style, language, and posturing of my coaches, but he did share with them an important belief in strong, silent masculinity. His silence lent credence to every coach who demonstrated such an approach to leading young men. I was nurtured in a culture that, by today's standards, would be considered abusive coaching.

THE LIABILITY OF OLD-SCHOOL COACHING

In early spring of 2013, a video of a Rutgers University basketball practice went viral. It showed head coach Mike Rice unleashing a barrage of violent, sexist, and homophobic insults. Acting like a boot camp commander, he used the threatening language of a middle-school boy, calling his players "faggot" and "fairy." The public learned that there were hours of such footage, indicating that this was routine behavior for Rice. Despite the fact that the players defended their coach, the general public was outraged and the negative exposure of the video led to his firing and the resignation of Tim Pernetti, the athletics director, for failing to take appropriate action after seeing the video.

When I saw the video for the first time, I thought of the endless number of football coaches I've encountered since I was eight who behaved in the very same way. Many were also physically abusive—twisting a player's face mask, pushing his chest, smacking his helmet to punctuate both negative and positive messages. They were not dissimilar from the guys who tried to haze me.

Frankly, Rice's behavior didn't shock me because it was so commonplace in sports. Perhaps his extraordinary petulance made him an extreme case, but in the world of football, the image of a raving-mad coach aligned with the violent nature of the sport itself. I believe Pernetti's failure to respond was similar to mine—we both reacted numbly because such coaching tactics were so familiar. We knew it was unacceptable, and yet we, perhaps reluctantly, agreed with it because it was all we knew.

I've talked with hundreds of coaches since the Rice video surfaced. In discussions about the culture and climate of their athletic department, I bring up the video and ask, "How many of you know 'that coach'?" Sheepishly, several hands will raise. Often, an uncomfortable tension immediately fills the air because "that coach" is right there in the room. Nobody judges him (or her) as a bad person or bad coach, and in many cases the behavior is not consistent with that person's demeanor away from sports.

Today, a cultural clash has surfaced around the value of old-school coaching. Many still liken the coaching style to a trusty old piece of equipment, kept around for nostalgia's sake, even though we question its effectiveness. For others, the old-school style and the nostalgia for it have the stench of an old locker. They argue that not only is the style ineffective, it has also become a legal liability and a danger to the safety and well-being of our children.

Revelations of the illegal, violent, and abhorrent behavior of athletes and coaches have become daily news. And with an ever-expanding audience scrutinizing every news sound bite and social media post, the ugliness of old-school coaching and the sports culture that condones it becomes more exposed. The Mike Rice video only confirmed what many critics of sports already believed: that they are a breeding ground for sexism, homophobia, and bullying. Rice was not an anomaly, nor was his behavior the worst violation of the vaunted title of coach.

THE CARNAGE OF HYPERBOLE AND MYTH

Prior to the victory over West Virginia that clinched our undefeated 1987 season, one of the greatest moments in my athletic life was beating the defending national champions and the team Syracusans loved to hate, Penn State. Before that, I had faced the Penn State defense twice, without much success. Their dominance was largely due to their brilliantly coached defense, for which Penn State was branded "Linebacker U." The architect of their defensive success was not Hall of Fame head coach Joe Paterno but the team's defensive coordinator, Jerry Sandusky.

In 2012, Sandusky was convicted on forty-five counts of child sexual abuse. Entering prison at sixty-eight years old, Sandusky will die in prison for the abominable crimes he committed in and around the football facilities at Penn State. Although he retired from coaching more than a dozen years before his conviction, he maintained privileged access to football facilities on campus. He maintained access due to his service with The Second Mile, a nonprofit he founded that served underprivileged youth. Like many patrician figures whom we fondly call "Coach," Sandusky's reputation was never in doubt. He was a source of pride for the school and community of State College, Pennsylvania, and was admired for the nurturing tutelage he provided to boys. The altruism people attributed to Sandusky, together with the vaunted benevolence of the Penn State football program, provided cover in plain sight for a pedophile like him to operate.

The response, or lack thereof, by Penn State's leadership to the assault led to charges of child endangerment for President Graham Spanier, Vice President Gary Schultz, and Director of Athletics Tim Curley, all of whom served time in jail. Their loyalty was not to Sandusky but to institutional reputation and a head coach who wanted to preserve his football program's credibility at any cost. Paterno died a few months before Sandusky's conviction.

The vehement condemnation of Joe Paterno, the school, and its culture of silence was warranted. The impact on the lives of the boys Sandusky assaulted will continue long after the next championship enables Penn State to "turn the page" as a football program. But we must not be distracted by a vigilante desire to focus all of our social outrage on the most obvious targets. We can't assume the culture *caused* Sandusky's behavior as much as it provided the perfect environment for him to operate. To this end, if we are going to anoint sports with a revered place in our society, it's critical that we scrutinize and hold to account the intent and behavior of all coaches. If the conclusion is that a pedophile in a football program can operate in plain sight, how many other dangerous messages are being conveyed throughout the field of sports?

A year after Jerry Sandusky's conviction, reports revealed that Miami Dolphin offensive lineman Jonathan Martin was leaving the team because he could no longer tolerate the excessive bullying by fellow lineman Richie Incognito. When the story surfaced, I found myself in the same situation I had during the Sandusky trial—in a car provided by CNN, headed into its New York headquarters to share my perspective on live television. This "bullying" story, as it came to be known, was perplexing for many because they could not imagine professional athletes bullying one another. Video and audio clips of Incognito's behavior left no doubt and exposed a deep hostility in the sports world, expressed through racism, sexism, and homophobia. And now, the very same media that helped accelerate the revenue growth of sports was exposing the greatest threat to its social credibility. Just before the car arrived at CNN, the driver asked, "Is there really bullying in the NFL?" I laughed. As I walked into the building, I thought, *They're finding out how sausage is made.*

In the mid-1990s, when I first considered how media was changing sports, I truly could not have foreseen the extent of its expansion and its ultimate impact. The tremendous financial success of the sports industry is a direct result of the speed, breadth, and depth of fan engagement through mobile media and technology. That same technology, however, has also exposed the darker sides of the business and personal lives of everyone involved, especially owners, coaches, and players like Incognito. Even with the existence of high-impact, multimillion-dollar marketing and branding strategies, the image of an individual or organization in sports is vulnerable to an unconstrained, anonymous public that is hungry for the next viral video or scandalous tweet. The major stakeholders in sports are engaged in a desperate, futile struggle to address the behavior and attitudes of individuals before they are exposed and cause damage to the entire business enterprise.

Meanwhile, the industry continues to perpetuate, promote, and protect the myth of masculinity by focusing on and highlighting the winner-take-all, zero-sum interpretation of competition. The narrow image of athletes, single-minded in their pursuit of victories, remains at the center of sports' cultural appeal and is inextricable from the hyperbole with which it continues to be presented.

While the industry churns on, focused on revenue generation, there are many in the sports world holding their breath, bracing for the next scandal and hoping it comes after their tenure. What is missing is a broad vision that focuses on the true development of young people through sports for the benefit of children, not the business. This requires a keen understanding of how warriors on the field were nurtured.

VULNERABLE WARRIORS

As media has revealed troubling aspects of the sports culture, we are also now witnessing the devastating impact on a generation of sports figures whose personal safety was ignored and neglected. Their psychological and physical deterioration is regularly on display. Men once considered invincible, like Wes Dove, who died in relative obscurity, are now obscure only because their deaths are all too common. To the sports world and the public, they were warriors who shaped football's image and its history, iconic symbols whose big moments not only entertained us but came to represent generations of American men. Now, they are the carnage of the hyperbole of sports, left in the wake of a mythical understanding of masculinity that depended on them for its validation, and of a business that continues to exploit their legacy.

We lionized these men and their teams. With nicknames like the "Doomsday Defense," the "Steel Curtain," and the

"Monsters of the Midway," they sacrificed their bodies for the game and for our entertainment. "Monsters of the Midway" was the name for the dominant defensive units of the Chicago Bears in the early 1940s; the name was restored in the 1980s by a former Bears player turned head coach, Mike Ditka.

One of the venerable tough guys in NFL history, Ditka is "old school" personified. But he also represents the dilemma presented by old-school attitudes and the myth of masculinity they perpetuate. As an elder statesmen of the game, he is an out-spoken advocate on behalf of former players physically suffering from the ill effects of the game. Although he has implored the NFL to take care of the men who have made the league such a success, in his job as an NFL analyst on ESPN, he's been less empathetic. When Ditka discussed the Miami Dolphins bully-ing story, he referred to Jonathan Martin as a "baby." He later stated that in his day, he would have taken Incognito to "fist city," suggesting that Martin should have assaulted his team-mate to resolve the issue.

Perhaps Ditka, known as "Iron Mike" during his playing days, was grandstanding for his ESPN audience and not actually promoting violence; however, he was articulating a sentiment that was readily received by a culture that accepts and often expects violence as a reasonable and appropriate response to any conflict, especially those involving athletes. For many observers, this was a predictable response from Ditka. Like my father's appreciation for the cold, blunt demeanor of organized crimi-nals, Ditka's bravado was consistent with the tough masculinity expected of coaches and athletes. But therein lies the insidious hypocrisy of old-school masculinity—we cannot have it both ways; we cannot continue to ask young men to "suck it up," "take it like a man," or solve problems by going to "fist city," but remain oblivious to the carnage that this perspective leaves in its wake. And we can no longer allow revered entities like sports to be free from our scrutiny as they advance violent, narrow definitions of masculinity.

When we fail to hold athletes accountable, such as a team of high school football players, for the heinous crimes they commit or fail to report, my faith in sports is shaken. And when sexual predators hide behind the hyperbole and myth of sports, I am less inclined to see sports as the positive and altruistic force that first emboldened me to speak my truth.

When I retired from football, removed from the process, I began to seek my true and authentic self, independent of the culture that provided me with an overinflated identity of privilege and power. I had to examine how the social construct of masculinity had shaped my identity. My process of reflection also had to include looking at masculinity independent from the issue of men's violence against women, to fully see how masculinity functions in the lives of *all* men. This revealed a profound paradox: sports were not just a stage for masculinity; they were also a hiding place for it. This realization uncovered a set of tremendously complex questions, the most fundamental of which was the following: if patriarchy is so powerful and privileged, *why* does it need to hide behind entities like sports, be portrayed hyperbolically, or rely on mythical identities to advance its purpose and bolster its status?

THE PIVOT TO SEEK HEALTHY
AND WHOLE MASCULINITY

The hyperbole of sports is not accidental, nor do I believe it to be malicious. The urgency to eradicate its harm requires a strict focus on the most egregious behavior of boys and men, but such a focus carries the risk of conflating "toxic masculinity" with being male, as if it is monolithic and other forms of masculinity cannot exist. Further, since men are disinclined to discuss masculinity as complex and gendered, or in ways that threaten to dismantle their power and privilege, the prevailing notion is that we have no choice but to reconcile with the factors contributing to our egregious behavior. This notion confines the discourse to positions that are often viewed as contentious, condescending, or simply not representative of most men. Subsequently, the dialogue becomes an exercise of awareness without growth.

To truly engage boys and men in a meaningful and sustainable dialogue, we must reject hyperbole, debunk the myth, and examine masculinity independent of the ways in which it garners attention—through its toxicity. In other words, we must seek a pure and authentic understanding of masculinity. Through a complex process steered by compassion, we need to make a pivot, in which we resist the temptation to prosecute unexamined masculinity in our culture. We must, for a moment, set down the fight against abuses of power and privilege, look beyond the carnage wrought by patriarchy, and engage in honest discourse about what it truly means to be a whole and healthy man.

4

Be a Man

TOMMY KANE

Forty-five minutes before addressing a college football team about sexual violence in November 2003, I learned that Tommy Kane had killed his wife, Tammara. My initial reaction was disbelief, and as I looked back on my years of work on domestic violence and sexual assault prevention, I reflected on countless similar stories. All the people in those stories had become characters—"perpetrators," "survivors," and "victims"—in one larger narrative that was painfully familiar and had no end. The story left me numbed, yet strengthened in my resolve not to succumb to feeling overwhelmed by the pain and futility of confronting such a heart-wrenching issue.

My disbelief also revealed a fundamental reason why confronting the issue is so daunting: we never want to believe that someone we actually know could commit such an unthinkable crime. Tommy Kane and I were teammates at Syracuse University. He was an extraordinarily talented wide receiver with quick feet and great hands. He was not very big and had a boyish face and charming smile. He was cool, he was slick. But he was not a murderer. From an intellectual and professional standpoint, I understood. But from an emotional one, I didn't want to face the fact that Tommy could kill his wife.

I compartmentalized the news about Tommy and talked

with the college football team. As we moved past the initial niceties and the conversation went deeper, each exchange made me think of Tommy. *Who in this audience is capable of this?* I wondered. *What comment by a player do I need to sharply rebuke to make them aware of the deep-seated misogyny and violence that could lead a student-athlete to kill?* In my head, I was conflicted. I wanted to allow these men their innocence and truth, but I also wanted to prevent the next "Tommy" from killing his girl-friend or wife. As an educator, I wanted to appear objective and detached about the issue, but I was literally shaking with anger and sadness for my teammate who I knew was sitting in a jail cell contemplating what he had done.

There I was, struggling to rationalize my personal feelings to fulfill my professional objective—as if they could actually be compartmentalized. As if "violent masculinity" was a category unto itself and my work was trying to get men to choose the right path: to be a good man rather than a murderer. This is far too often the approach—encouraging positive outcomes by highlighting the negative alternatives. We point to the horrific and extreme cases and hold them up as what not to do. This is not an effective method of teaching prevention because we typically only identify with what is most familiar to us, not the most extreme boundaries of human behavior.

I did not find myself thinking about Tammara's funeral. Instead, I imagined sitting in that jail cell with my teammate Tommy, wondering, *How did we get here?*

ROOTS OF MEN'S VIOLENCE

Violent masculinity has been so normalized through sports, en-tertainment, and the evening news that we are often incapable of tracing its roots to a more innocent place. Our cultural un-derstanding is also clouded by the rigidly defined roles we give to men who execute the violence: Athletes are "warriors" who have proved their mettle through determination and grit. Violent criminals are inhumane monsters unworthy of "a place in decent society," while depictions of them in TV and film serve our gratuitous need for villains. As extreme manifestations of violent masculinity, they maintain precarious positions. We observe them from safe distances, to witness or be entertained by the performance of violent masculinity, which feels so foreign to us that we cannot fully understand its depth. As a result, such extremes are disassociated from the innocent vulnerability of boys and our everyday humanity.

Tracing violent masculinity to its roots is an uncomfortable process and can be compared to unearthing secrets in our family trees. We are reluctant to see violent men as once-innocent little boys, or to consider the socialization process that fomented their rage and propensity to hurt others. However, if we as a society fail to do so, we not only fail the boys who will someday become perpetrators of violence, but we fail to make an honest attempt at fulfilling our collective goal to "stop the violence."

I couldn't believe the news about Tommy because I was reluctant to trace his violence to a time of innocence that he and I once shared. As young athletes, neither of us were characterized as violent or physically intimidating, yet we blended in and thrived in a sports culture steeped in the rhetoric and threat of physical force. I can say unequivocally that the culture did not directly *cause* Tommy's violence, but it did foster greater acceptance of rigid and hostile interpretations of masculinity.

Understanding Tommy's behavior would require a deeper dive into his life's history, which rarely occurs. Once he committed that lethal act, he went from "violent athlete who entertains us" to "violent felon," not worthy of our consideration or analysis of his complex past. Somewhere in the midst of the violent masculinity that we lionize or turn to for entertainment are the traces of an innocent masculinity that, for so many boys, is cultivated into something else. We must look closer in order to understand why part of being a man includes the inevitability of violence.

THE BOY IN THE AIRPORT

Following a few days of lectures and workshops on college campuses, I had to wait for a delayed flight in the Atlanta airport. My only diversion was watching a woman and her three-year-old son who were also waiting for a flight. I empathized with her as she struggled to rein in his energy and curiosity. He was "working the room," taking advantage of every object he could find, turning the airport terminal into a playground. The luggage carts became skateboards and each chair a launching point to the next one. I laughed to myself, wondering how long it would be until his mom snapped.

Initially, she was gentle and patient, but each reprimand further limited his exploration. When I sensed they were reaching the inevitable impasse, I began to focus on her, wondering what her breaking point would look like and what language she would use, knowing she was in a crowded terminal. She continued to wear him down with sweet reminders as he, in turn, grew bored and frustrated and began to whine . . . then cry. This made me laugh again because I totally understood his tears. (I wanted nothing more than to get out of that terminal as well.) Apparently, his crying was the breaking point, and the mother exclaimed, "Will you be a man!"

What is he supposed to do with that? I thought. The smile left my face as I watched him stop crying, comport himself, lower his head, and sit quietly with an icy grimace on his face. In an instant, with one command, the cute, energetic boy morphed into a "little man," sitting stoically, indifferent to his emotions.

In that moment, my mind returned to the several groups of college men I had worked with in the preceding days. The members of such groups have disparate backgrounds and come from different corners of the country and the world. Sports and higher education are what bring them together. And when I arrive, with few exceptions, it's the very first time any of them discuss masculinity and men's violence against women, yet despite that fact and their varied backgrounds, they have an immediate consensus on what it means to be a man. While keeping my focus on the ultimate goal of stemming men's violence against women, I fixate on the solidarity men find around certain aspects of their masculine identity. That solidarity sits at the root of men's violent behavior in all its forms, even if they themselves are not violent.

Although the frequency of discussion about men's violence against women has dramatically increased since I began working in the field in the mid-1990s, the content of the conversation hasn't changed much. What remains are uncomfortable truths and unanswered questions about the role of men . . . and the innocent boys they once were. Boys are not born violent perpetrators; violence is learned behavior. But when and how is it learned? And how has it been so normalized that we fail to even recognize the need for examination?

Watching the boy in the airport play with boundless innocence and curiosity was rejuvenating. But when the charge to "be a man" shut him down, I found myself scrutinizing the very *process* of how narrow masculinity is learned. I was used to the notion of adult men learning to accept masculinity as a fixed thing, "as is," but here I was brought face-to-face with the forging of narrow masculinity in a child. It was both heartbreaking and enlightening.

I immediately recognized the dissonant message behind the charge: he was simultaneously empowered and silenced. I vividly saw the complexities of masculinity and the ways it is, quite frankly, confusing, especially for a young boy who was a long way from becoming a man. He was equally distant from being a violent perpetrator. This marked the beginning of my thinking on the pivot we need to make, one in which we engage boys and men in a more intimate and aspirational manner. As I boarded my flight, I thought more deeply about the specific language the mother used, as well as the tacit messages she conveyed. She did not say, "Ignore your feelings" or "Your feelings don't matter." This may not have even been what she meant, but those messages were certainly received immediately. Judging by how quickly the little boy stifled his emotions, he had learned the lesson long before that day in the airport. From infancy, he had developed his definition of masculinity by observing older men and hearing statements like, "Be a man," "Man up," and "Big boys don't cry."

When a three-year-old is crying or whining, he is expressing feelings that attentive adults need to decipher, no matter how annoying those feelings are or how incongruent they are with parental expectations. Adults' responses to those expressions will shape his understanding of and relationship with his emotions. If we discourage boys' expression of their emotions, they will learn to suppress, ignore, and ultimately distrust their feelings. This was, after all, the intention of the mother's command: to shut down the demonstration of his feelings so *she* didn't have to deal with them.

"Be a man" is also a hollow demand founded on an unfair assumption, which is that the boy (or man) to whom it is directed understands and agrees to society's narrow, fixed definition of masculinity. If a boy does not demonstrate and live by that strict definition, we ask, "What is wrong with him?" This ignores the truth of how a boy or man truly and authentically understands himself beyond narrow and superficial social expectations. There is nothing *wrong* with him if his personal identity empowers him to live beyond the limits of social and cultural expectations.

If the boy in the airport is never allowed to experience his feelings, how will he learn to deal with complex situations that require careful consideration of his actions or the myriad personal stresses he will surely encounter? How will he ever learn to be empathetic if he himself does not understand how to feel? He will, in fact, be in a perpetual state of *reacting* to situations, without the emotional tools needed to effectively guide him. He will ultimately be conditioned to create a wall around himself that is far too familiar to many men and women.

THE MANDATE

In this interpretation of masculinity, "the wall" is often hailed as a virtue. The expectation that men *not* do something—that is, express their emotions—is quite unnatural and can be confusing. This isn't a definition of manhood that boys grow into naturally—it's what I call the *mandate* of masculinity, and typically it is established at an arbitrary moment when boys are suddenly required to prove their manhood, demonstrating what they have observed or been directly told. The result is the "little man" that we regularly challenge boys to be in order to meet adult expectations and interpretations of male behavior. And, like the boy's mom in the airport, we adults have no patience for negotiation, as the mandate provides the boy no room for discussion or compromise with us or with his peers.

The pressure to be a "little man" shatters the innocence of childhood and comes at the expense of some of the most important qualities of our humanity and loving relationships—vulnerability, empathy, and emotional competency. Sadly, this pressure is usually applied early in life, by the family members whom boys trust and upon whom they depend for love and support. I distinctly remember the night I decided that giving my dad a kiss good night is not what "big boys" do. I also remember him asking me why. Ironically, I knew that being a big boy meant I didn't have to give him a reason. I had achieved the appropriate degree of emotional distance that was familiar to men in our family. While there may have been a measure of pride in my "coming of age," it arrived at the expense of the intimacy in our relationship. And it was never spoken of again.

The hardening of emotionless masculinity is often fostered by those in close relationship and proximity to boys: family members who they trust. This is an early example of how the definition of masculinity is layered with blind spots. We falsely equate the increase in emotional distance between a boy and loved ones with his growth and maturity as a man, reinforcing the notion that emotional expression is unnecessary. In the beginning, the process can be confusing for young boys, but through trial-and-error experience, most young men eventually understand societal expectations. Men generally believe boys should learn as they did—the hard way, by just figuring it out. Although many may *want* to identify with a broader understanding of themselves, their restrained outward expression impairs their modeling of healthy behavior for young boys, perpetuating a cycle that sets boys adrift without concrete alternatives to the nebulous, flawed messages they receive from adult men.

This process lacks the standard expectations we have in other areas where competency in core skills is paramount. Do we adopt a position that core skills aren't important when our children learn to drive? Would that be satisfactory preparation for your child's teachers? Would you hire a person who learned and functioned that way to deliver your baby or redo your kitchen? With regard to how we nurture boys into manhood, we must provide a purposeful and comprehensive vision of what it truly means to be a whole man, a whole person. This includes a deliberate approach to teaching boys to think and act as emotional beings.

THE BOX OF MASCULINITY

In the late 1970s, a group known as the Oakland Men's Project (OMP) was founded. Their work, in many ways, has provided today's activists a tether to an unabridged understanding of masculinity, one not tainted by popular opinion or the mainstream media. The OMP was organized to explore the crisis of masculinity and understand the role that its toxic interpretations played in fostering a culture of misogyny and sexism. However, the OMP also understood the burden this ideology had on men, and their focus was as much on helping and supporting men as it was on protecting women by dismantling patriarchy. This is an important distinction because it sheds light on how our current discussion of masculinity is typically in the context of the violence men commit against women, not violence in general or violence against men. This speaks to an inherent sense of chivalry that is uncomfortably condescending to women as well as men. The underlying assumption is that the only purpose of examining masculinity is for men to fulfill their duty to protect women, and that men's emotional health is secondary to that duty.

One fundamental tool the OMP created was the "Act Like a Man Box." An illustrative teaching tool, the box is often used by advocates and educators as a metaphor to describe the narrow confines of masculine identity and the limits on its emotional expression. To create the box, you draw a square and fill it with words that describe qualities of what it means to be a man ("tough," "strong," "athletic," "aggressive," "provider," "protector," and so on). The box provides a visual explanation of masculinity, rendering men to a confined space of limited expression and identity. The implication is that we should aspire to get out of the box or eliminate its walls and think critically about the most salient qualities in the box.

In this discussion with men, we only interrogate the toxicity and negative ways in which the qualities in the box manifest in men's lives. This does not represent the reality of all men and works to deepen the myth of what a "real man" is supposed to be—leaving men with a binary choice (real man or less than a man) and indicts the ideology to which men have been raised to aspire.

Since it was created in the late 1970s, the "box" has been widely used by antiviolence educators and activists to identify the angst and toxicity of men's transgressions. Consequently, the original intent of the box—to illuminate how masculinity is defined and governed—has been conflated with "toxic masculinity" and men's violence (against women). However, the box does very little to inform us how to envision and achieve the wholeness of men and masculinity.

It is important to note that there is nothing wrong with being tough, strong, or even emotionally guarded when appropriate. I believe men must not seek to get out of the box but to add to its content, expanding how masculinity is defined. Further, and more to the point, men need to access, embrace, and learn to use all the qualities of our humanity that we have otherwise been conditioned to ignore.

THE TOOLBOX

Like many of my colleagues, I have used the box exercise thousands of times in nearly three decades, but it has consistently left me feeling a bit empty. There is always a glaring omission of the truth about the men in the room, myself included, that is as profound and universal as the narrow responses men provide. Don't we possess the qualities of whole, loving humanity, yet are only choosing to deny them? How should the discussion be reframed so that men realize and actualize their wholeness?

These questions led me to reimagine the box of masculinity as a toolbox that men carry, containing the emotional tools that enable us and guide how we function as whole people. But because men are raised without a full expression of emotions, we learn to function by using very few tools in our "box." Here the expression "If your only tool is a hammer, then everything is a nail" is apropos.

Our vulnerability and empathy are essential tools for fully understanding ourselves and engaging with others. But since men are raised not to acknowledge or give credence to those emotions, they learn to function without them. They carry the entire box and feel its weight yet utilize very few of the tools. However, the fact that men function in this way does not eliminate the possibility of them using the full range of their emotions stored in their subconscious (toolbox). They constantly and deliberately suppress and mask feelings in response to social expectations that require emotional competence. In spite of this behavior, many men will thrive in a culture that rewards men's emotional reticence; they enjoy privilege they don't see and celebrate success in prescribed ways. The weight of the box becomes a burden and often results in the ultimate blind spot of masculinity: the avoidance of self-care, where failure to address personal health, depression, and anxiety can lead to destructive behaviors.

Each emotional tool serves a purpose. As an athlete, my

emotional tools included an insecurity in my abilities and fear of my opponent. I embraced that vulnerability and turned it into honest self-assessment and respect for my opponent. This made me prepare smarter, work harder, and truly appreciate the experience of competition.

Mastery of emotional tools *is* the very definition of emotional intelligence and should be treated like any other set of skills we expect boys to learn as they grow and mature. Helping them embrace, interpret, and utilize these tools will enable them to conduct their lives with an honesty that begins with an authentic wholeness within themselves.

THE LIE OF MASCULINITY

The celebration of excellence in professional sports is also the celebration of a narrow and mostly untenable interpretation of masculinity. Such an interpretation needs a champion, someone whom the culture can point to and declare, "*There* is the successful realization of masculinity." This is, in part, why athletes are referred to as role models even though they are arguably the public figures whom we know the least about in a meaningful way. As I stated earlier, this was my situation: the more successful I was as an athlete, the more I became a caricature—a narrow interpretation of successful masculinity. Of course, this assessment isn't ever stated overtly, only tacitly. It's part of the insidious nature of what I call the *lie* of masculinity, served by the hyperbole of sports.

Some contend that sports are merely a diversion from the mundane routines of our lives, but if that were true, they would not evoke such fervent tribalism or inspire so many fans to reserve their "Sunday prayer" for their team. At the center of most of this fanaticism are male athletes whose identities are reduced to the warriors we intrinsically need them to be.

I spent many years of my life representing this interpretation of "successful" masculinity. As an athlete, I thrived in the lie of masculinity and it supported my privilege. This lie is part of a broad narrative that subtly discredits men whose lives are, by contrast, defined by caring, vulnerable, and sensitive love, or simply by the absence of "real man" bravado. My very presence made the comparison tangible. There were many instances when I was unaware of the impact that I had on people around me; I was reinforcing narrow expectations and setting a distorted example for younger men. To them I was a "trusted man," a "good guy," and I'm certain they never considered the lie of masculinity I was helping to perpetuate.

During my years as a "celebrity athlete," my mere presence perpetuated the lie in countless instances. At the time, it felt like I was merely being used as a tool to raise money for charity or to promote the business. However, there was something deeper at play that is central to the lie of masculinity and patriarchal privilege.

I can recall a charity golf outing when I was part of a group that included a preteen boy whose father had paid for the opportunity to play with a professional athlete (me). Through the afternoon, I heard a barrage of sexist, homophobic jokes and innuendos, and though I tried, I could not successfully address the rote behavior of men gathered in the absence of women. Later I understood that my mere presence actually reinforced the lie of masculinity and other troubling attitudes. I was accidentally helping to validate the sexism, misogyny, and homophobia with my presence as a professional athlete, an icon of narrow and privileged masculinity. That was what the men in the group paid for: the opportunity to be up close with a male sports celebrity. The interaction made me "real" and confirmed the ways in which we are not dissimilar as men. For the boy, I was an affirmation that sexism and homophobia are a part of masculine identity. In very specific ways, the lie of masculinity, along with the culture of patriarchy and the hyperbole of sports, was being directly passed through me to another generation of men.

THE PROMISE OF MASCULINITY

I did not know the men on the golf course that day. And they did not know me. Yet we fell into predictable roles, the performance of which was based on shared assumptions on what it means to be a man. Holding that performance together was the *promise* of masculinity and the fear of losing the privilege it offers.

The promise of masculinity is conferred by patriarchy and supervised by our immediate peer group of men. It's guaranteed as long as boys and men remain loyal to the fixed rules of the mandate of masculinity. Different groups of men set their own nuanced expectations of their members. For example, in financial circles the promise is based on the unbridled pursuit of wealth; or in bodybuilding circles, on the purity of muscle development. In many ways, the privileges of the group become secondary to conformity and solidarity. All members don't have to achieve perfection or even success, but they must adhere to the group's doctrine.

The concept of the alpha male, the archetype of dominant masculinity, is dependent on subservient men in his orbit validating and legitimizing his dominance. The image and persona he represents empower the group to aspire to that archetype, even if he does not fully possess all of its qualities. In fact, many of the privileges associated with the *promise* are never realized but remain part of the myth and serve to uphold it. And since the mandate is so strict and unforgiving, the fear of being ostracized is immense and foreboding. This is both a burden and another blind spot governing the lives of men, and it is prevalent across almost every social group, including those organized by race, religion, class, geography, and generation.

THE PERFORMANCE OF MASCULINITY

Before they can achieve male privilege, men must demonstrate the qualities it embodies. This is the *performance* set by masculinity's mandate. We carry out this performance unaware of how living in such a way comes at the expense of those around us who must bend to the conditions that make our lives so simple. One of the reasons men reject the notion of male privilege is because most are terribly insecure about the unrealistic interpretation of masculinity that gives them power; it's an interpretation they don't expect to ever actually embody.

Think of the person you know who is always working to portray himself as something he is not, and the great efforts and lengths he goes to prove his wealth and success. His life is a facade made up of ostentatious language, behavior, and spending to "buy" legitimacy and approval, no matter the cost. In isolation, his life is modest; however, around others who are vying for the same identity or material status, he is exorbitant and becomes a caricature. This is exactly how the lie of masculinity ultimately becomes the performance of masculinity—rather than living the reality of their complete and authentic selves, men act to maintain a certain perception for the approval of other men.

This is another role athletes serve in perpetuating the myth of masculinity—they become our culture's alpha males, ideal surrogates for what the promise of masculinity looks like in its most grotesque form. They are revered for sacrificing personal well-being in the name of winning for the team, community, or school. Helping to support the myth is the affiliation fans have with their team, which authorizes and encourages overt displays of passion. Through sports, men can and do display a variety of emotions, but only in the context of caring about their team. And that caring is demonstrated in the ways sports allow men to safely express their vulnerabilities as "superstitions" and their insecurities as hatred for the rival team. "Man caves," those rooms where sports are widely celebrated, are "safe spaces" for the expression of vulnerable identity. They also represent men's primal need to be seen and loved by other men and to gain their approval.

Men's devotion to their sports team is not folly; it reveals a greater truth: all men *do* care about a lot of things and are vulnerable in many ways. But we are rarely encouraged to demonstrate the breadth of this truth. Contrary to the belief that men act out to impress women, the truth is that we often behave in certain ways to impress other men. And the closer men are to their immediate peer group (of fellow athletes, fraternity brothers, male professional colleagues, etc.), the more acute and strict the rules of that performance become. The authentic identity of boys and men is that we are loving, caring, sensitive, and vulnerable—that is, we are human. But our peer groups control the rules of the performance and the path toward validation.

The costs of the performance of masculinity are many. I've alluded to how it comes at the expense of those around us. It also wages immense costs directly on us, particularly because we are forced to act as though we are impervious to pain. As we are seeing with professional athletes today, the impact of such a myth can have a devastating impact.

THE NECESSITY OF PAIN
In 1983, just before the first game of my college football career, I experienced my first serious sports injury. I had been hurt sev-

eral times in the preceding eight years of playing, but never severe enough to miss a game. The same week I attended my first
class at Syracuse University, I had surgery on my left knee and
was put in a plaster cast from hip to toe. Following the year-long
rehabilitation, I finally made it back on the field, only to sustain
the worst injury of my entire career—a third-degree separation of
my left shoulder. It was another season-ending injury and the
most excruciating physical pain I have ever experienced.

My initial response to both injuries was disbelief. It was
disorienting to be told by a doctor that the severity of my injury
had rendered the decision to play no longer my own. What *was*
familiar was the physical pain, though it was inconsequential
because I was conditioned to ignore it. "Know the difference
between pain and injury" was a mantra that I used in order
to steamroll through every other painful moment in my athletic career. During my last year of college football, our team
T-shirt read, *Disregard all extraneous stimuli!* That's exactly what
we called pain. *No pain, no gain. What doesn't kill you makes
you stronger. Pain is fear leaving the body.* These messages are all
part of how masculinity is performed and how the promise of
masculinity is earned in the world of sports, for athletes and
those who admire their grit and toughness. As part of the hyperbole of sports, these messages are among the first lies we tell
ourselves.

It's critical to note that my dramatic sports-injury stories are
also part of the hyperbole of sports. Such stories have greater social
significance as society has grown less brutal and more genteel.
As a venue known for high risk of injury, sports provide ample
opportunities for athletes to overcome pain and thus demonstrate their masculine bona fides.

During an appearance on the television program *60 Minutes*,
legendary NFL coach Bill Parcells expressed part of his philos-

ophy as a coach. "Don't tell me about the pain, show me the baby," he told journalist Mike Wallace. "I don't want to hear about the process." Aside from the fact that no man should ever use this analogy, this is an astute example of how pain is necessary and how individuals like Parcells ignore it in an attempt to assign deeper meaning to the hyperbole. Parcells disregards pain because he equates it with weakness. However, in sports, the "pain" is a process that *is* critical to the endeavor—preparation through meticulous attention to detail is done *pain*stakingly, and it constitutes the overwhelming majority of an athlete's time. Parcells's career in football spanned more than half a century and he won only two championships. He is a member of the Pro Football Hall of Fame and one of the most successful and respected coaches and executives in league history. As special as those two championships may have been, the experiences, relationships, and true love of the game through the process are what he likely values most about his career.

Part of what made Bill Parcells a great coach was his unwavering demeanor. His approach was loved by players, hated by the media, and idolized by the fans of other teams who wanted *their* team to embody the same inflexible disposition. For the show that is the NFL, this was great theater. Yet the notion that we can or should ignore the process (and with it, the pain) is not just unrealistic, it's perilously flawed.

In 2002, while studying the brain of former Pittsburgh Steeler player Mike Webster, Dr. Bennet Omalu made what would ultimately be one of the most consequential discoveries in the game of football and sports in general. It was a newly named condition known as chronic traumatic encephalopathy, or CTE, characterized as deterioration of the brain due to chronic trauma to the head. In other words, the degeneration is not caused by a single hit or concussion but the cumulative effect of repeated and untreated head trauma. Subsequent to the discovery, "concussion protocols" have been implemented at all levels of sport. These require team staff to recognize head trauma when it happens and that athletes immediately cease play to allow the brain time to heal. In other words, we are acknowledging the process and asking athletes not to ignore the pain but tell us about it.

Despite the tremendous risk in ignoring the pain, this practice of responding to it remains difficult for many athletes, just as it was for me, despite how painful my season-ending injury was. Admitting or succumbing to pain, or any sign of weakness or vulnerability, is completely antithetical to how we are taught to behave as athletes and, more acutely, as men. In fact, while concussion protocols have become a reality, athletes who openly acknowledge pain are still often criticized by certain men (often sports pundits, announcers, and fans) not simply because they expect athletes to endure pain, but because remaining indifferent to it is an ingrained hallmark of masculinity. An inability to "fight through it" or mask it completely is often a disqualifier for alpha male status.

Just as unaddressed physical pain has a cumulative impact, unaddressed mental and emotional pain has a cumulative impact as well, in both athletes and men in general. In such cases, a stoic attitude is typically the best result we can hope for. More often we see risky behavior, violence, and a general affinity for violent culture as the effects of ignored emotional pain and trauma. Not only does this distort an individual's perspective of care, it also dictates how care (and empathy) are extended to others.

WE DON'T RAISE BOYS TO BE MEN

When I first started to probe this issue, I asked the question,

"What does it mean to 'be a man'?" with very few presumptions. Admittedly, I was insecure about what parts of my identity I might expose and fearful of being accountable to those qualities and emotions that I was just beginning to access—being openly sensitive, loving, nurturing, and empathetic. But since I was on a mission to prevent men's violence against women, I was eager for ways to connect with men, and I realized I could use my self-examination as an effective lever to earnestly engage them, regardless of their demographics. The more I probed, the more I came to realize that across all populations, *we don't raise boys to be men, we raise them* not *to be women or gay men.*

In other words, as I have detailed in this chapter, we do not raise boys to be whole, loving men but instead give them a *mandate* to exhibit certain qualities, to enact a *performance* of masculinity that is actually a *lie* only serving to support and maintain patriarchy. Masculinity is delivered as an uncompromising and even hostile juxtaposition to the identity and lives of girls and women.

Although male privilege is real, men in general do not understand or recognize it because they do not recognize masculinity as a gendered force in their lives. They only understand the unrelenting burden of maintaining behaviors imposed upon them as men. For those who feel the burden of maintaining such a position, one that seems both unnatural and tenuous, it is hard for them to see that they are privileged, especially if that privilege never provides relief from their burden.

The lack of a thorough examination of gender and masculinity has consequences beyond the emotionally limited ways in which men view themselves. To acknowledge their masculinity would be to cede control of the qualities of being a man to some nebulous set of social circumstances. Men believe that if they do not recognize gender, then they can maintain a control in their lives that is not governed by something they don't understand. This is the fundamental challenge to women's fight for gender equity: if men don't acknowledge or understand themselves as gendered beings, there is no plane on which equality with women can exist.

In all the universe, men have more in common with women than any other entity, yet we draw the most rigid line of distinction when comparing the two groups. A boy or a man can be favorably compared to an inanimate object or animal ("He's built like a house," "He's my dog," "He runs like a deer"), but if he is compared to a girl or woman, it is often the ultimate insult. This is misogyny. And the fear of being the object of that offensive comparison is one of the dynamics that establishes prevailing notions of masculinity.

Further, during the process in which boys learn about masculinity by watching Dad, they also learn that copying the behavior of Mom is unacceptable and will subject them to sharp scorn. Along with shaping the narrow ideology of masculinity, this process simultaneously establishes in them a disrespect and animosity toward girls and women.

While I maintain that the work of "the pivot" must be about nurturing the emotional health and wholeness of boys and men, it remains critical to address how notions of masculinity have a detrimental impact on girls and women. Until we raise boys to live in their authentic wholeness, we will continue to be tasked with the daunting challenges of fixing broken men and protecting the women they encounter.

You Throw Like a Girl

PACIFIST MEETS MISOGYNY

It was 1975. I was ten years old and had just transferred from Our Lady of Lourdes School to a public middle school. Sidney Crawford was my first friend in my new school and, before I knew it, also my first fight. When Sidney landed the first blow, the ringing in my head seemed more perverse than the fight itself. Once it started, I had no choice but to physically defend myself.

As a crowd of fifth-graders gathered around, I became unsure who was a spectator and who was a potential "second puncher." Like most middle school fights, the "boxing" portion didn't last long. Within seconds, Sidney and I were rolling in gravel, wrestling for the dominant position: one on top of the other, knees pressed against opponent's shoulders and crotch in his face. As the chanting and screams of our classmates grew muffled and distant, I thought I was going to pass out. The crowd parted briefly enough for me to catch my breath and allow Miss Dyches, the school disciplinarian, to swoop in and grab us by the backs of our collars like puppies. As Miss Dyches dragged us to her office, Sidney, who seemed strangely familiar with her, was honest and contrite: "I'm sorry, Miss Dyches, I got in another fight."

Sidney and I had started the day as friends but at some

point, during recess, we began throwing rocks at each other. Initially, it was fun trying to dodge each other's rocks, but when we started adding commentary and epithets like "sissy" and "fag," the rocks became stinging exclamation points to each insulting word. Just before the first punch, I remember Sidney saying, "I ain't no sissy!" I had touched a nerve. Like most kids, I understood how such language was hurtful. What I didn't fully understand was why. At just ten years old, why and how did we learn to respond so decisively and in physical ways to certain language? We didn't even understand the true meaning of the words but knew that we should not tolerate being called them. We were just reacting and, in the process, demonstrating the way in which the violent behavior of boys is rooted in sexism and misogyny.

But our behavior was so normal that it was barely noticed. Miss Dyches handled us with the efficiency of law enforcement processing an arrest. We were booked, given detention, and sent back to class. My heart was still pounding, my face sweating, and thoughts of what would happen after school occupied my mind. However, if it were not for the whispers and pointing of fingers by other students, I would have thought I was the only one to experience the altercation. From the adults, I sensed nothing but indifference. They had seen it before. *Boys will be boys*.

The truth was that the conflict was driven more by the ideology of boys *not* being girls. Sidney and I were not trying to establish who was "boy enough"; instead, we were fighting in defense against being associated with girls.

I had never been in a fight before that day and, at age ten, I had an instant realization—I didn't like fighting and never wanted to do it again. It's clear I was a pacifist at an early age and I remember how absurd that choice seemed at the time. I hated the subsequent, ever-present threat of violence that was a part of being a boy. Something I had learned, separate from my disdain for violence, dealt with the performance of masculinity: I learned that my reaction to the fight was critically important; I had to appear nonchalant in the face of violence. My response to the fight was more important than my performance in it, in that simply being willing to fight and subsequently show indifference had greater value than actually "winning" the fight. Sidney and I were friends again by the end of the day, and other than the notation in Miss Dyches's daily ledger, there was no evidence of the scuffle or lasting animosity between us. But the impact of misogyny and sexism that bonded us, though imperceptible, was profound.

There was nothing particularly compelling about my fight with Sidney Crawford. In fact, it was outstanding how ordinary it actually was. Sidney and I were on a playground, standing our ground and staking our claim as "king of the hill." The reaction from adults only confirmed that our behavior was expected. There was no real follow-up about what led to our lunchtime skirmish; in terms of misbehavior, it was comparable to being late for class or missing homework; it was accepted as inevitable and even expected. However, if our fight had been examined more closely, what triggered it would have been revealed.

There were plenty of other insults Sidney and I could have traded with each other. I had just transferred from Catholic school, he was shorter than me, and I doubt either one of us knew how to dress ourselves with any sense of style. However, when I called him a "sissy," I purposefully evoked the universal nemesis of all boys—*girls*. Sidney's response was immediate and unequivocal.

Misogyny is defined as the "hatred, dislike, or mistrust of women, or prejudice against women." The word itself often elicits knee-jerk, animated responses from men who assert the contrary by expressing their passionate love for women. The performance of masculinity in this case is not the overt demonstration of hatred toward women, but it encompasses a multitude of attitudes and behaviors stemming from the misogyny embedded in our masculine identity. Although linking the performance of masculinity to a hatred for women may seem illogical, the behavior of boys and men tells a different story. Drawing that link is really just as "illogical" as a ten-year-old pacifist rolling in the gravel, trying to punch his new best friend. Even when the misogyny planted deeply in our masculinity triggers men's destructive behavior, our responses don't delve into a gendered analysis. We simply fall back on a sexist refrain—*Boys will be boys*.

The language Sidney and I used to insult each other was clearly degrading to girls. But to assume our violent behavior was inevitable and the product of our innate pathology is degrading to boys as well, and it illustrates the low expectations society has for them. This is what I call "simultaneous sexism": it has an explicit impact on the lives of women and girls, as revealed through the work of feminists over decades, but it also hurts boys and men. And the impact on them is rarely, if ever, examined.

THE ULTIMATE INSULT

For several years after college, during my involvement with the student-athlete leadership team program, I worked with elementary school children who were the same age as Sidney and me on the day we fought. Ironically, the fight never came up in discussions during those years. It was not until I began working with college-age and older men on issues specifically related to men's violence against women that I recalled the incident. Once again I was twenty-nine years old and just beginning to deconstruct the social forces of gender and masculinity on my life. Working with men forced me to examine the innocent days of my youth to better consider the origins of those forces. It also led me to probe deeper together with other men, which included asking them to name the worst insult they heard as little boys, during the most innocent period of their lives.

The consensus in their responses, across every demographic, and to this day, is striking. Though they may not use the same verbiage, they invariably say the ultimate insult is being equated or likened to a girl in any way. No matter how it is delivered—as a taunt, insult, or challenge—to do anything "like a girl" indicates inferior maleness. Their responses are sometimes visceral because of the relevance this dynamic maintains in their lives today. The ensuing conversation galvanizes them around their collective experiences as men and their uneasiness about acknowledging their inherent sexism.

Applying this conversation to a time of innocence helps men consider the truth about sexism and misogyny without being defensive. While the ultimate goal is to understand the depth and impact of misogyny, it's also critically important to identify the innocuous way it becomes entrenched. To that end, in the course of this discussion I typically ask if they have seen *The Sandlot*, a 1993 film about nine boys and their love of baseball, set in a suburban California town in the summer of 1962. It is a feel-good story that evokes the playful innocence of boyhood. When I mention the film, it eases the tension of discussing sexual violence. The response is always warm, with the mere mention of the film filling the room with youthful silliness. And as if on cue, someone will shout, "You play ball like a girl!"—a direct quote from one of the film's most memorable scenes. We may not all identify with baseball, suburban

California, or the year 1962, but the familiar moment arrives when the innocence of boyhood is confronted by its nemesis. The boys' greatest opponent is not another team but the charge of association with girls.

The sandlot boys were innocent and seemed to only care about one thing: baseball. They competed against no opponent, just for the love of play. But the dramatic moment happens when a group of boys from a neighboring town arrive to the sandlot and challenge them to a game. The two teams line up against each other, chests puffed out in a faux-intimidating pose, and launch into a barrage of insults that at first are gender neutral. Laughter and chants stoke the confidence of the loudest players, until one of the sandlot boys throws down the gauntlet and levies the ultimate insult, "You play ball like girl!" It lands like a physical blow and changes the entire dynamic of the scene. The music stops, and stunned faces indicate a crucial line has been crossed. The only way to resolve the standoff is by playing baseball. It's time for action!

The scene is salient for me in two significant ways. First, it's a harsh, complicated expression of sexism against a backdrop of innocent, virtuous Americana, which makes it easy to overlook and not examine critically. Second, the boys' sexist message is delivered in the absence of girls or women, which helps illustrate how boys are often socialized. It generally happens in contexts where traditionally feminine qualities and viewpoints cannot be considered; this advances and cements assumptions.

The timing of the film's release was fortuitous. It was just a year before I arrived in Boston to work with Jackson Katz and the MVP team, and was initially challenged to understand my own socialization as a man and how that informed my view of women. Personally, I began to learn from Jackson and so many other social justice leaders and educators. But I was being tasked with translating the complexities of sexism and misogyny while simultaneously deconstructing masculinity *and* its links to sexual and domestic violence. And that felt overwhelming, especially because I was in the middle of my own self-examination. This was further complicated by the limitation of having to deliver that message in a sixty-minute lecture to college-age men. I needed to find a common point of reference with men, from which we could process through constructive dialogue the machinations of sexism and misogyny in our lives and see how they shaped attitudes and behaviors around men's violence against women.

THE LANGUAGE OF MISOGYNY

"You Throw Like a Girl" became the title of the lecture I have delivered on college campuses since 1998. As an insult, it is arguably one of the most aggressive assaults on the psyche of boys and men. And it is a quintessential example of simultaneous sexism. Boys suffer because the insult demands a decisive response that also diminishes them. They are forced to express the narrowly defined qualities of the box of masculinity—that they are tough and emotionless and their allegiance lies with the promise of masculinity. The significance of this experience on the overall health and well-being of boys cannot be overstated because the effects of these early-life behaviors and the formation of attitudes about themselves literally last a lifetime.

The language is direct and purposeful as it creates solidarity among boys by enlisting them in a position against girls. Further, it establishes the belief that girls and women are "less than." Early in my work, I called this the "language of sports" because of its pervasiveness in that world, but it is universal in our society. As boys grow up, "You throw like a girl" devolves into targeted and crude epithets like "pussy," "bitch," and "faggot." A direct line can be drawn between these kinds of verbal assaults and men's attitudes about, and subsequent violence against, women. If we categorically believe that another group of people are "less than," we are more likely to disregard them in a multitude of ways and to negate their feelings and rights. We are also more likely to stand by idly in the face of mistreatment and violence. It is hard to separate the culpability of men in general when the (silent) majority tolerate the behavior of those responsible for commiting the violence.

When some boys choose to stand up for girls and women, social pressures often discredit their intentions. Such advocacy will attract a litany of insults that question their masculinity and, most importantly, their solidarity with other boys. The intensity of the pressure varies by situation, but general consensus suggests that concern for the rights and safety of girls and women is below the interests of boys and men. Outside of protecting one's daughter, the notion of supporting women's issues is relatively nonexistent in the discourse among men. The very fact that we call such matters "*women's* issues" prompts reflexive postures ranging from indifference to defensive hostility.

Most people would agree that teaching sexual violence or even hostility toward women is not the goal of such language. They generally assume that it's most often used with positive intentions. It's a challenge voiced among men to achieve great things or in the spirit of rivalry and competition, just as "innocently" used in *The Sandlot*. Nonetheless, the message for boys is clear, and the language helps establish strong opinions about the inherent value of girls—that they are inconsequential and their overall behavior and interests are trivial. If degrading a boy comes from comparing him to a girl, then he'll want no association with girls and will do whatever it takes to dispel any notion that he is like them. Respect for girls is lost without even interacting with them. Many boys learn to reject all things feminine, and as they mature, the divide widens between their masculine identity and the qualities associated with women such as vulnerability and empathy.

In the early stages of their development, these formative lessons for boys don't immediately manifest as problematic behavior. At an age where social and emotional differences emerge, boys may express their slight distaste for girls and vice versa. But any real threat of mistreatment can be easily mitigated if parents and other adults recognize the socializing influence of language and the attitudes and behaviors that precede and perpetuate violence, just as adults could have recognized the sexism and misogyny in the interactions between Sidney and me that anticipated our violent behavior.

Unfortunately, the "boys will be boys" mind-set usually prevails, allowing boys' unhealthy attitudes to advance into the teen years and adulthood, during which they intensify and lead to more troubling behavior. For example, when a young boy hits or is physically rough with a girl, adults often excuse the behavior as his way of expressing affection, essentially saying, "He hurts you because he likes you." The message this sends to girls is obvious and disturbing, while the message to boys is equally disturbing since it suggests he is incapable of appropriately conveying feelings of affection. It also reveals a reluctance on the part of adults to nurture the wholeness of boys. Moreover, it implies that he is not required to ever learn how to express himself appropriately. He doesn't have to dig into his emotional toolbox for the purpose of expressing his feelings in healthy, nondestructive ways.

At some moment in a boy's life, the presence of girls provokes his greatest dilemma to that point. He has to reconcile the dissonance between what he has learned about girls with the innate feelings he has for them. Solving this puzzle is not simply about navigating dating or relating to girls as intimate partners, but understanding the role girls play as it applies to the mandate of masculinity. In boys' early interactions, girls serve to fulfill a part of the mandate that tells boys that being a man is the demonstration of power and control over girls and women, as well as a kind of sexual prowess devoid of any emotional vulnerability or connection. Whoever is the first boy in a group with the courage to simply talk to a girl, he often demonstrates it with a cool indifference.

Even when boys take an aloof posture with girls, they betray an innate craving for connection and love. But after being taught not to express emotions or appreciation for girls and then discovering an attraction to them, with the expectation of engaging with them intimately, they are left with a trail of inadequate explanations for how to do so. It becomes difficult and confusing to manage what they've learned and what feels natural as a person. This is not just with regard to girls but within themselves as boys. They've learned not to appreciate female characteristics, yet have those characteristics themselves. And after learning to use phrases like "You throw like a girl" and worse, they are told to treat girls and women with respect and as equals in the classroom, workplace, and at home? There is no real social movement to help them navigate and resolve these dilemmas in healthy and productive ways.

THE IRONY OF THE PERFORMANCE

The performance of masculinity contains a profound irony: although the essence of our humanity is that we are tough, strong, and aggressive, *and* vulnerable, sensitive, and dependent, our performance is an exaggeration of the former in order to mask the latter. This applies directly to men's relationships with women. Many believe men's violence is not only inevitable but necessary as a protective instinct. Some will further suggest that tough, violent masculinity is a function of testosterone, the hard-wiring of our DNA for our own survival and the protection of others.

But aren't strength and courage best defined by confronting our vulnerabilities and dealing with them, rather than ignoring conflict or adversity, hiding from each encounter, with our emotions tucked away? Surely, if we have to defend against an imminent threat, we have the right to call upon our physical prowess and even do so with force. But in recognizing there are some things worth protecting, don't we also reveal our vulnerable humanity? Don't we convey that we hold loved ones and cherished values dear in our hearts and that they give our lives meaning and purpose?

Another piece of the irony of the performance is that we have been conditioned to categorically disrespect women yet care about them passionately. We have been raised to ignore our own feelings and understand women as being "less than" in part because we perceive their expressiveness as a sign of weakness. They unavoidably become a mirror of our own humanity and evoke the disdain we have for our own vulnerability.

In the mandate, there is no more venerable role than the chivalrous and gallant protection of the women in our lives. Hard-wired or socially learned, the defense and protection of women to whom we are most vulnerable is one of the first lessons of the mandate. Sadly, it is also when men subtly experience the first woman they understand to be "less than."

When I ask men the worst insult they can remember as little boys, other than being compared to a girl, they say any insult of their mothers or mere insinuation about them. Although "momma jokes" have long been mainstream and considered harmless fun in many circles, they are rooted in the notion that

women are in need of protection and it's the role of men to provide it. At an early age, boys demonstrate this understanding of
dutiful and protective masculinity in their attitudes about their
mothers, which is why momma jokes are so provocative.

When I ask men if "daddy jokes" would be as provocative,
the answer is almost universally the same: "No, because my
dad can take care himself." It is in this response that I came to
understand one of the most unsettling ways that misogyny is
deeply rooted in masculine identity. Our mothers are the first
women we learn to see as "less than." Yes, our *mothers*, who
nurture and care for us and often control nearly every aspect
of our lives. As boys, many of us are told that she requires the
physical protection of the "little man" in the house. This may be
presented innocently as chivalry, but when the same protection
is not applied to his father, we conclude on a fundamental level
that Mom is less capable than Dad. This also cements the role
of men as protectors.

To be clear about this point, boys don't necessarily understand what "protect" or "take care" of Mom means in their role
as the "little man," but they do understand the physical obliga-
tion in those narrowly defined terms. They are not encouraged
to be wholly *supportive* of Mom, but to physically *protect* her. To
be supportive would require adopting a broader interpretation
that recognizes those duties for which it's assumed are her responsibility and concern (namely, women's issues). Many boys
learn a limited role in maintaining and supporting the household, and, as a result, are relegated to a more elemental position
as "guardians at the gate." In reality, this typically results in boys
being tasked with killing spiders and carrying the heaviest bag
of groceries rather than actually providing protection from a
real threat.

Clearly this process does not take place in every household

or for every boy, but to varying degrees, every boy who moves beyond the nurturing care of his mother and toward personal independence must reconcile with the emotional detachment prescribed by the mandate of masculinity (lest he be labeled a "momma's boy"). This can be a confusing time as boys search for independence by ignoring their emotional selves to seek validation from a patriarchal culture. Boys will not only detach from their emotions but from the girls and women who can access those emotions, and those relationships will push them further from their own emotions because of the need to control the intensity of those feelings. They are ill-prepared or discouraged from expressing feelings, which are evoked by those they love.

As boys mature and the rules of masculinity grow more rigid, it can lead to them feeling an unspoken sense of isolation—of being alone with the fact that they lack the permission or ability to express themselves fully, and of being forced to deal with the complexities of life while lacking a mastery of the emotional tools they carry. This can lead to a troubling place where emotional angst collides with the rigidity of masculine identity and expression, culminating in violent behavior.

INEVITABLE VIOLENCE
AND PROTECTIVE PATRIARCHY

In a society held together by laws and social structures created by men, there is an incentive for men as well as women to advance and uphold patriarchy, even when it manifests in destructive ways. People accept violence as inevitable and even promote its use for the sake of maintaining order. I call this the rationale of "protective patriarchy," the same one that argues that a strong military fosters peace. Lethal force is justified—if you are on the right side of the violence.

However, when violence does not serve the dominant group,

it's swiftly called a grotesque display of inhumanity and vilified in ways that divert our attention from a true examination of its origins in privileged masculinity. We are quick to blame the victim, or we incessantly argue about gun control, mental health, and radicalization. Or we call perpetrators "monsters," likening them to the ghosts and whatever unknown forces feed our hardened, irrational fears. Mired in the morass and debate, we fail to confront hard truths about patriarchy and masculinity.

In regard to men's violence against women, one hard truth people ignore is how protective masculinity is used to mask misogyny. And nowhere is this more prevalent than in the confounding relationship between many dads and their daughters. Long before girls reach dating age, most fathers consider in very specific terms the safety of their daughters around boys. For some, it literally begins when the child's sex is determined in utero. He begins to talk about having his "hands full" protecting his little girl. The disturbing underlying message is that girls are objects and "prey" in a world controlled by their only natural "predator."

The father becomes the proverbial "protective dad" who is driven by fear, guilt, or redemption, and he vigilantly surveils his daughter's relationships while striking an intimidating posture. In this familiar narrative, a popular trope is the father cleaning his shotgun in front of a boy who wishes to date his daughter. It's part of an explicit affirmation of the inevitability of men's violence, including the violent protection of women and girls.

Fathers' attitudes are shaped when they are very young. The "little man" directed to "take care of your mother" becomes the father who implores another man to "take care of my little girl." He thus never escapes the utilitarian dimension of his masculinity. I am not questioning the paternal instinct to protect one's child, but since many dads don't have the same protective behaviors with their sons, what messages are they subtly conveying to their daughters about personal autonomy, privacy, and the role of men in their lives? At what point do girls and women no longer require the physical protection of their fathers or the men to whom their fathers "transfer" that responsibility? And when will men lay down this burden of "protection" and learn to live lives of love and caring, recognizing the family dynamic as a shared egalitarian experience?

The protective-dad narrative also perpetuates the notion that a woman's safety, empowerment, and even her identity are derived through her relationships with a man. This is the other edge of the protective patriarchal sword: the insidious notion that renders her always vulnerable to his inevitable violence. In fact, most men who are violent toward women do so once trust and safety have been established in a relationship. The deeper the trust, the more sustained the violence becomes. It's a noxious intersection of several elements: the trust and belief many women have in men's dutiful, protective masculinity; men's emotional angst; and the rigidity of their masculine identity and expression. What results is a violent eruption that occurs "for her own good" or because he "loves her." She *made* him do it by usurping his privileged authority or by not recognizing a passion in him that is so intense that he is ill-equipped to understand or control it.

When men violate the fundamental role of "protectors" and perpetrate violence *against* a woman, the excuse for his behavior reveals the intrinsic misogyny that says it's his responsibility to protect *his* woman. The examination of his behavior is selective and feckless. What remains more uniform in our reaction is that women are blamed and their behavior is scrutinized before we search for pathologies in the behavior of men.

WHY DOES HE STAY?

In September 2013, a video became public showing NFL running back Ray Rice punching his girlfriend Janay Palmer, leaving her unconscious on the floor of an Atlantic City casino elevator. Due to Rice's celebrity status, the video became the center of a national spectacle and a sad, sobering account of men's violence against women. The footage made it indisputable: by using physical violence to resolve an argument, Rice betrayed the trust of his partner in a loving and committed relationship.

The video, which was released seven months after the attack, silenced those who initially attempted to diminish its brutality, some even raising doubt that an assault had actually occurred. For those who were quick to indict and discard another violent black athlete, it was easy to label him a bad man who deserved harsh consequences. Yet, when the media frenzy slowed, it became clear that the outrage was selective. Only those who cared about Rice's football career or the issue of domestic violence had a sustained and cogent interest.

When Janay Palmer agreed to marry Rice, the conversation splintered into different camps. Regarding this private matter in the public discourse, after all, she had forgiven him, and public opinion should have no bearing on her decision or their lives. This was especially true for those who had an interest in using her story to support their larger agenda. For instance, when Janay Palmer appeared in a press event convened by the Baltimore Ravens and expressed regret and culpability for *her* "role . . . in the incident," it was done at the behest of the Ravens organization and in the interest of Rice's football career. We can assume that the Ravens fans following the press event generally accepted the inevitability of men's violence against women. They were concerned only about the fate of their running back.

But to the domestic violence prevention community, her

statement appeared forced. It was as if she were apologizing for failing to remain subservient, or saying that she should not have "provoked" him, knowing he would inevitably be violent; that his passion was so intense, he was like the little boy who hits girls to express affection. While there was some recognition of the blatant "victim blaming" of the press event, it was the omission of an explanation for Ray's behavior following the incident that stood out to me. It was a hard truth that was either ignored or at least not thoroughly considered. Whereas privileged patriarchy dictated that we wonder why Janay Rice stayed in an abusive relationship, we failed to examine why Rice himself stayed in the relationship. This is precisely the way in which sexism harms men and perpetuates unproductive strategies of addressing the problem.

One of the more significant threads in the responses to Palmer's decision to marry Rice was from women around the world who saw themselves in this situation. Via social media, these women articulated "why they stayed" in relationships with men who routinely hurt them. They provided a litany of social, emotional, legal, and economic pressures they faced, as well as pressures in the form of oppressive cultural norms. They stayed, in part, because they were socialized to rely on the protection of men and the patriarchal decorum and financial structures that supported men in providing that protection. For women, the clear penalty for violating or being disloyal to protective patriarchy serves as an outright threat to their safety and autonomy, and it is a prime example of how patriarchy is an oppressive force in their lives.

In contrast to the public conversation about Palmer, the one about Ray Rice was centered on his football career. The consequences to his actions were limited to his playing career and, following his release from the Ravens, the question of which team in the NFL "needs a running back" and if he was worth the risk. There was little interest in understanding Rice as a person. People dismissed the assault as "uncharacteristic" and a "mistake." They also pointed out that Palmer and Rice were in a fight preceding the punch he delivered, as if that served as an adequate explanation.

Ray Rice is not a monster and his violence was not a "mistake." He is a successful man, nurtured by a culture that does not teach men how to express their feelings or embrace their vulnerability. Again, it's a culture that considers violence an essential and unavoidable element of masculinity, and in this case, it simply found its trigger.

Rice and Palmer got married in the midst of the media and legal firestorm surrounding them. It is clear he genuinely loves and cares for her. I cite their story not to interrogate their relationship but to expose the social discourse around such situations that is unproductive and designed to allow privileged patriarchy to go unexamined. In all our public debate about *what* happened, we never delved into *why*. Why would Ray Rice act so uncharacteristically—throw away his career and hurt the woman he loves? For those who saw him only as an NFL player, the behavior was either inevitable and therefore predictable, or it was random and senseless. It was as illogical as a ten-year-old pacifist rolling in the gravel as he fought his new best friend.

The public discourse paid little attention to Rice's violation of his fiancée's trust and, more poignantly, completely failed in dissecting the question of why *he* stayed. Why did he or why does *any* man stay in a relationship where threats, abuse, and violence are part of how he functions as a partner? And why do our public and private conversations ignore this question? If patriarchy is teaching our girls to expect and even depend on the inevitability of men's violence, either as a force to protect them or to hurt them, then what is it teaching our boys?

The privileged patriarchy allows men to be silent about these questions as well as many other matters of intimacy and personal relationships. We are not expected to have cogent, rational, and deeply considered views on caring relationships and emotional fulfillment. Our privilege allows us to choose silence and indifference over accountability and responsibility to our partners and ourselves; we laud the strong, silent type and see others who express themselves in emotional or nuanced ways as being effeminate or not "real men."

The voices and perspectives of women traumatized by violence have defined the narrative about abusive relationships. Again, until men engage in an honest dialogue that recognizes masculinity as a gendered phenomenon, gender violence will remain a one-sided issue. Moreover, we cannot continually expect women to bear the scars *and* responsibility of abusive relationships alone.

A Men's Issue

MEN'S PRIVILEGE = WOMEN'S PROBLEM

On April 30, 1992, in Burlington, Ontario, the naked and life-less body of a fifteen-year-old girl was found in a roadside ditch. Kristen French was the most recent victim of one of the most horrific and unimaginable series of rapes and murders in Canadian history. Paul Bernardo, later identified as the "Scarborough Rapist," was responsible for nearly two dozen rapes dating back to the late 1980s. This time he was aided by his wife, Karla Homolka, in abducting, raping, and killing French. Less than a year earlier, the couple had murdered and dismembered fourteen-year-old Leslie Mahaffy, another Burlington resident. Mahaffy and French were the second and third victims of a grisly and disturbing rape and murder spree that began with Homolka's own younger sister, Tammy.

In the summer of 1992, during my second season in the Canadian Football League, I lived in a luxury apartment in the center of Burlington, a quiet upscale suburb of Toronto. A block from my apartment was a strip of restaurants, shops, and hotels that lined the shore of Lake Ontario. That's where I spent most of my nonfootball hours. My favorite place was a restaurant with an energetic and festive atmosphere and a staff composed mostly of college-age women, many of whom I considered friends. One afternoon, someone spotted a vehicle that fit the description of the one in which Kristen French was abducted. It was parked in the lot adjacent to the restaurant. The anxiety in the room was palpable. The young women, typically carefree and free-spirited, now wore nervous scowls of paranoia and trauma.

I didn't understand why they were so visibly upset or even concerned. It was a beautiful sunny afternoon and the restaurant, where virtually everyone knew each other, was quiet. They were safe. At least, that's what I thought. They did not feel safe and, in fact, would not be truly safe until Bernardo and Homolka were positively identified, apprehended, and put behind bars. Still, their concern and my lack thereof revealed the way in which men's privilege is invisible, along with the constant threat of sexual violence that women endure.

That car in the parking lot was a chilling reminder that *he* was unidentified and still "out there," possibly nearby. I was both incapable and disinclined to see it from their perspective. The fear of a sexual predator was not something I considered. I inherently knew that I was not the target—not because I was a large man, a black man, or a famous man. I was simply a man. A sadistic serial murderer was loose in my neighborhood, and I felt no alarm, no threat; I did not alter my behavior, modify my schedule, or change my daily habits. In no way did I consider my personal safety. *He* was not after me. However, the reality for my female friends was dramatically different. There was a profound amount of privilege in my ignorance and lack of empathy in that moment.

In 1992, I was oblivious to that privilege. The threat of violence to women may not always be as extreme as in this terrible case, but it is always there. This is what makes sexual violence different from most violent crimes—it has a disproportionate effect on half of the population. And men's silence and indifference regarding this issue only intensifies the perceived threat and further isolates women.

Bernardo and Homolka were arrested in 1993. The following year, I retired from the CFL and my perspective about men's violence against women was starting to shift dramatically. As the story in Canada unfolded, with the couple's eventual conviction by 1995, my understanding of their crimes evolved quickly. During that time, I also began to recall the countless women I knew who had experienced violence as well as the moments in my life when the issue of men's violence against women paralyzed the world of women around me but did not affect me at all. I was struck by this most profound manifestation of male privilege—that not only did those crimes not affect my life, but I easily forgot them. These were life-shattering events for women, yet to me they were simply a "shame" or an "unfortunate event" or, to put it bluntly, "some fucked-up shit." That was the extent of my empathy and outrage. As I have written, if we are honest about the fact that the overwhelming number of perpetrators of violence against women are men, then we need to be more deliberate and specific with our language by calling it "*men's* violence against women." We must stop using passive language and referring to it as a "women's issue." Our "issues" have become women's problems. We must regard men's violence against women as a "men's issue," and it is from that perspective that we must examine the problem and search for solutions.

As a man, I am on the same side as the aggressor in men's violence against women—I have more in common with the male perpetrators, including those who rape and murder, than I do with all women. This is not to say I share values with these men, nor is it to say that men can't be victims of violence perpetrated by other men, but I do share the privilege of a patriarchal culture that produces and remains relatively silent about all forms of men's violence against women. Men who are not violent, abusive sociopaths and are even considered "good guys" still support perpetrators' behavior through their silence and failure to address the cultural influences we all share.

THE LIST

Privilege is often difficult to acknowledge for those who have it because it is invisible in our everyday lives and we may not be actively or purposefully applying it. We are not exposed to the reality others experience each day, so we lack a true understanding of it. Being oblivious to the hardships of others does not necessarily make one feel better off; however, that doesn't make the unfairness of privilege any less real for those who don't have it.

When I heard about the murders of French and Mahaffy, I found them gruesome and sad, but they were also just news stories, as distant from my life as a weather forecast for another part of the country. The news didn't provoke any change regarding what I wore or where I parked. When that car appeared in the parking lot of my favorite restaurant, it did not trigger a set of protective behaviors I had been conditioned to adopt in my life, as it did for every woman there. In fact, it appeared as though they were suffering from PTSD. Their conditioned responses kicked in, and as their workday ended, they vigilantly executed a whole set of safety protocols.

In my workshops, I often present the following question to women and men: *What do you do on a daily basis to protect yourself from being sexually harassed, sexually assaulted, or raped?* While their responses show that some experiences vary along the gender spectrum, by and large they illustrate the profoundly diametrical differences of our experiences as men and women when it comes to personal safety.

It's a prompt I inherited from Jackson Katz. The first time I heard him ask that question, I immediately felt guilt, not just because of the privilege of not having to worry about being sexually assaulted, but also because of the countless times that that privilege—invisible to me—triggered a fear and anxiety in my friends that I did not understand, even when there was potentially a murderer in the parking lot. In the years since, I have used that simple question to help men experience a similar realization. When I ask the question, it's not uncommon to hear mocking laughter. Others, intending to retort with anything that defends the male position, explain the things they do to avoid conflict or a physical attack. However, when we delve further, it becomes clear that while men do, at times, anticipate violence, they are expecting it from other men and it's rarely of a sexual nature. The reality is that we almost never do anything to protect ourselves sexually, and to consider the question is to acknowledge something so foreign and distant from our experiences that many men find it laughable.

Conversely, when I pose that same question to women, I'm flooded with responses:

> *Carry mace or pepper spray.*
> *Only park in well-lit areas.*
> *Take self-defense courses.*
> *Carry keys between your knuckles as a weapon.*
> *Never leave a drink unattended.*
> *Check the backseat of the car before getting in.*
> *Learn to use various weapons (including firearms).*

From there, the discussion expands into strategies that women employ in a multitude of situations, from benign and routine to scary and threatening moments, when they were necessary.

Most men know the list; we've heard our fathers caution our sisters, and we ourselves may sternly recite these instructions with women we know and for whom we care. And in the twenty-plus years I have been asking that question, the list has remained the same—it features the strategies, tools, and warnings women have been inundated with since they were young girls. It's also consistent across every demographic of American culture. Again, as familiar as the list is to men, we rarely consider the psychological impact for women of having to heed the list and live with the problem of sexual violence as if it is theirs alone.

NOT MY PROBLEM

It is possible for men to engage in productive conversations about men's violence against women. Unfortunately, they are often compelled to engage only in the aftermath of an assault. In this case, two factors stand in the way of an honest discussion and productive work toward solutions.

First, men are prone to take a defensive position. We are reluctant to see ourselves in the crime, the details of which always sound beyond reasonable behavior when they are considered from a distance. And the specific details of a case are routinely limited and often get muddled in the public debate. Further, the discussion often focuses on a single moment in time—the rape or assault—instead of the broader context, which can include precipitating factors and the history of behaviors and interactions that shed light on the incident.

Second, because the conversation happens *after* an incident, men inevitably assume that the conversation is only happening because she "spoke out"—bucking the cultural pressures that have kept women silent—or she did not adhere to "the list," which would have kept her from imminent danger and helped her extract herself from a bad relationship or situation.

Any sanction placed on men in general, including discussing the larger issue, becomes directly attributed to her disclosure or her poor judgment.

In my discussions about certain cases against men, I have heard from some men who were actually annoyed—at *her*. *She* was the one who ruined their day by forcing them to talk about the issue. In effect, they blamed her for jeopardizing their privilege or status simply by refusing to remain silent, much in the same way the victims in the horrific hazing case at Mepham High School were blamed for the cancellation of the team's football season. These are examples of men blaming the victim while not examining the actual problem and culture that created the perpetrator in the first place.

SEMANTICS OF SEXISM

Language is another way we preserve patriarchy, cloaking the fact that sexual violence is overwhelmingly committed by men against women. Such violence is often described in gender-neutral terms like "crimes of passion" and "domestic disputes." Or sexual violence is presented as a misunderstanding of intimacy, such as when rape is referred to as "nonconsensual sex" or "date rape." This language whitewashes men, absolving them of direct culpability, and suggests women are complicit in their victimization.

Prior to meeting Jackson, I had been involved in prevention programs in secondary and elementary schools for nearly a decade. I had come to understand how limiting the word "prevention" can be in this field of work. Prevention work is typically triage to a larger issue and most often risk reduction or avoidance instructions. We typically only respond to a particular event by assessing and developing strategies to prevent "that incident" from happening again. (I am reminded of this strategy each time I take off my shoes at the airport.) Most prevention efforts apply a "continuum of risk reduction," with the focus on those at greatest risk of victimization. Ultimately, this is counterproductive because it does not provide solutions but instead maintains a focus only on those who are potentially most adversely and profoundly impacted. We base solutions on the experience and perspective of victims, as if *their* experience is the source of the problem.

The language we use about incidents of men's violence against women both blames and stigmatizes them. Based on the work of the late feminist linguist Julia Penelope, Jackson calls it the "semantics of sexism," and it goes like this:

Jack beats Jill.
Jill was beaten by Jack.
Jill was beaten.
Jill is a battered woman.

Jack was the one who committed the assault. No matter what precipitated the crime, *that* is what we must prosecute and prevent from reoccurring. But because we are quick to dismiss him as a social deviant, a monster who can't be understood, his pathology is not scrutinized. In fact, he has been totally removed from the conversation. This is also an example of how sexism and patriarchy hurt *men*; Jack's violence is normalized. The assumed inevitability of his behavior makes it easy to discard him but also prevents us from helping him address the pathologies that led to his violence. This is also part of the blind spot of masculinity that fails to see Jack's humanity. If we were to ask *why* Jack beats Jill, we could understand his personal history and how his attitudes and beliefs were learned and supported. We could then develop strategies to mitigate those influences on his behavior and apply those lessons to how we educate and raise boys.

Instead, we become solely focused on Jill and scrutinize her behavior, right down to what she was wearing at the time of the attack. We gawk at her body much as we would at a crime scene, like rubberneckers slowly passing a highway car accident, pausing to witness the destruction caused by Jack. In its passive construction, "Jill was beaten" is similar to "She got pregnant," and it is consistent with the general way we discuss men's violence against women. We passively give approval to the inevitability of (men's) violence by citing crime statistics without even mentioning men:

1 in 4 women is sexually assaulted.
Every 15 seconds a woman is abused.
Four times a day a woman is murdered.

We never talk about how many *men* per second or per day commit acts of violence against women. Nor do we talk about how those men are often acquaintances of women. In fact, about 80 percent of sexual assault cases are perpetrated by men who are not strangers. Therefore, the "list" and those tactics designed to prevent the sudden "stranger attack" do very little to protect a women at risk of assault by friends or partners. "The list" provides a false sense of security and agency for women who have been told that they can protect themselves in a culture that has done nothing to address the behavior of men. This is the essence of rape culture.

This paradigm that says the onus is on women to avoid men's violence is beyond disingenuous: it's dangerous. It is passed on to successive generations and has become the subtext of the prevention strategies disseminated by social justice and violence prevention organizations, schools, and government entities. Ultimately, it provides a false understanding that such behaviors will protect girls and women.

ACCUSER AS PERPETRATOR:
HER TRUTH BECOMES THE CRIME

In recent years, greater levels of activism and media scrutiny, along with the lever of social media, have exposed the pervasiveness and brutality of men's violence against women. The increased scrutiny also reveals how attitudes and language distort the narrative about violence to preserve patriarchal values and privilege.

With the assault cases that receive the most media attention, the perpetrator is often a celebrity athlete or entertainer who does not readily fit our understanding of the easily discarded "monster." The success he has achieved serves as a form of defense for him; patriarchal culture assumes highly achieved masculine success is benevolent because it supports our understanding of normalcy and righteousness. In the cases of those we admire such as an athlete or entertainer, we create another layer of defensive disassociation from his crimes as we personally identify with the qualities he possesses and want them for ourselves; we blind ourselves to his potential to commit assault.

A separate standard works against the woman. In an attempt to be "fair" to the male perpetrator or portray a more "balanced account," victims of violence who report the crime are summarily called the "accuser." This term subtly casts doubt about whether or not the assault actually occurred. She is not necessarily viewed as the aggressor in the crime, but it's her insistence that the crime be prosecuted that becomes central to the story, because she has disclosed what we would otherwise simply ignore or be uninformed about. Her report is a challenge and an affront to male privilege and the status quo. He, in turn, becomes the "victim" of an accusation that may threaten his privilege and cause damage to his reputation, social status, or professional position. It is also often intimated that she has an ulterior motive, as if she has something to gain in making the accusation.

According to US law, alleged offenders are innocent until proven guilty. This is a reasonable principle in the court system; however, in today's media-filled and overly scrutinized culture, those defending "alleged" perpetrators can include industries and individual organizations attempting to preserve a veil of security, safety, or ethical and moral integrity. The defense is not always of an individual's rights but can also be on behalf of a brand or institutional reputation.

In many cases, when women publicly come forward with sexual assault accusations, they do so in direct opposition to large, formidable institutions supported by patriarchal economic interests. And in the cases involving athletes, women may find themselves at odds with a large academic institution, a popular professional sports team, or an entire sports league. This means that they are facing not only their perpetrator but whatever multibillion-dollar industry stands behind him. Few individuals can successfully take on an opposition with that kind of legal, financial, and media leverage.

When it comes to sports, there is yet another powerful force looking to silence the woman accuser: the fans and alumni who don't want to see their star player benched or their team's reputation damaged. They are often unconcerned with the moral accountability of the universities or corporations behind those teams. Prone to extreme prejudice, they also stand behind a rhetoric that nothing matters but winning at all costs, so their position quite often exceeds the bounds of decent humanity. In some horrific cases, some will even wish ill will and death upon the women who expose their heroes.

LOW EXPECTATIONS

We're all familiar with the standard victim-blaming tropes:

How a woman is dressed stands as a plausible justification that she was "asking for it." (To be clear, to endorse that thinking is to believe that a woman would intentionally choose certain clothing in the hopes of prompting a sexual assault.) If she was drunk or left a party or bar alone, then her decision-making skills should be questioned; if she struck first before an assault, then she got what was coming to her. People are finally recognizing the perniciousness of these rationalizations, though they fail to also notice how they reveal low expectations for men as evolved beings.

As long as tired defenses of male perpetrators continue to be considered and applied, they will remain categorical insults to *all* men. And as long as men legitimize this thinking in jokes or through their failure to speak out against such claims, *all* men should be considered accomplices of rape culture.

We have to ask: Are we really totally incapable of self-control? Are we animals requiring leashes or muzzles? One of the first excuses for condoning men's violence is the notion that he "just snapped," and usually (as the excuses go) because *she* went too far, hit him first, provoked him, or "pushed his buttons." Yet these excuses completely contradict the culture that nurtures masculinity. In the hypercompetitive world in which men live every day, we are constantly challenged by other men; the entire performance of masculinity is rooted in proving that masculine mettle in a multitude of ways. Facing adversity and challenges, being strong, and maintaining control are fundamental qualities of the performance. I remember coaches who would grab me by the face mask and literally spit in my face as they would berate me with insults I would not tolerate from anyone else, in any other context. On those occasions, I did not "snap" or lose control. My restraint was not just a testament of my will to ignore my feelings and deny my own dignity; it also emerged from the risk assessment I made in the moment. The consequences of hitting my coach, my boss, or my male friend were far greater than hitting a woman or girlfriend. In many cases a man doesn't "snap," he simply understands that hitting a woman is his authoritative right, for which there are very few consequences. In some small circles, he may even receive praise for "handling his business" or controlling "his woman."

These profoundly disturbing assumptions are also prevalent in men's responses to facing rejection from women. To be clear, rejection can take many forms. It can be as momentous as leaving a marriage or other long-term relationship and as minor as rebuffing a man's overtures. In either extreme, women regularly endure hostile and even violent responses. In cases of long-term relationships that are abusive, women are at greatest risk of murder when they leave. And if a woman denies a man's advances, no matter how she handles it, she can be subjected to being called a "bitch," among other things—as if her worth is determined by the man who acknowledges her.

Ironically, for men who react this way, it is their own self-worth that is in question. Insecure in their masculine identity, they are dependent on women's affirmation of them. Rejection from women pushes them into the narrowness of their identity. With no other recourse to reconcile their privileged masculinity, they lash out with an abusive retort or behave like a petulant child who doesn't get the toy he wanted.

He covets her one moment, placing her on the pedestal he's designed; but she is immediately devalued and relegated to a position of being "less than" if she declines to be the treasured item to which he has given his attention. This is also an insidious element of "protective patriarchy" where a women's identity and worth are determined by a man. Women raised in this paradigm will be apprehensive to reject a man's advances in anticipation of his hostile response, and this legitimizes his anger and loss of power and control (of her).

COLLEGE MEN

This analysis may come across as the critique of a liberal feminist bent on dismantling men's power. While this may be partially true, my intent, as I have said, is to protect men as well as women. In a rapidly evolving society, the risk of men not keeping pace increases the more we remain silent about these complex dynamics. That risk is the blind spot of privilege. Our silence stems from the assumption that this is a women's issue and men are unaffected. Our inaction results in a lack of growth and development of young men, leaving them more vulnerable to the repercussions of their behavior by a society that is evolving without them.

Since the mid-1990s, I have been involved in a robust conversation with college men that has been both edifying and productive. College men are consumed with performing the masculinity in which they were nurtured; they are both unapologetic and understandably naive about patriarchal privilege. Further, they are supported by (academic) institutions that may be defined as liberal but are exceptionally conservative in how they function and operate. This provides an interesting lens through which to examine masculinity and men's violence against women.

When I began my work in this field, it was situated in the larger context of domestic violence and sexual assault educators, researchers, and advocates who were considering interpersonal and relationship violence on a broad scale. But I found that college student culture was unique and defined by a vulnerable innocence that presented some challenges but also led to keen insights on this global problem, because while the academy works to maintain an egalitarian environment, the values of the larger culture still permeate campus life, thereby revealing certain truths about gender-based violence.

The preponderance of the violence is evident in all corners of our society—law enforcement, the medical community, the military, educational institutions, and wherever men and women have to coexist and function together. But of all these environments, none is more vulnerable or challenged than college campuses. And no environment demands more scrutiny.

In 2007, one of the worst shootings in US history to date occurred on a college campus. On April 16, Seung-Hui Cho killed thirty-two people and wounded seventeen at Virginia Tech University. The attack brought into question the safety of college campuses, where now it seemed any anonymous individual could just wander in to start a killing spree. However, Cho was not a stranger to Virginia Tech, he was a senior student. This made his rampage even more troubling—he was in some sense a needle in the haystack in this college community of more than thirty thousand students.

College campuses have always been challenged in reconciling the freedoms of movement and expression with the concerns for physical safety. However, in recent years the most aggressive public safety position that higher education has taken has not centered on defending against a mass shooter. The real safety imperative has been protecting one group of students, essentially half of the student population, against the other half. Complicating that imperative is the fact that the "dangerous" part of the population, in most cases, dominates higher education's social and cultural identity.

Campus environments are designed to foster a liberal education that allows for intellectual exploration. As such, it's natural to assume that gender equity would be among higher education's top priorities. Women now represent the majority of college students, including in law schools, where in 2016 women outnumbered men for the first time. In large part this has been made possible by legal mandates such as Title IX, which prohibits sex discrimination by any educational institution that receives federal assistance, and other levers fostering gender equity in higher education. Yet many campuses continue to struggle to fully rid themselves of the sexism and misogyny that once assumed women did not belong on campus. The sexism was imperceptible because women were not present, but today, many founding values and traditions still exist throughout higher education, especially in social and cultural ways.

Long-standing college traditions serve as powerful reminders that much of campus life is still dominated by male privilege. One such tradition, homecoming, is wrapped around football—the sport that is the 800-pound gorilla in the fight for gender equity. In student social life, the Greek system also reflects privileged masculinity, with fraternities controlling much of the social scene on campus. This is largely bolstered by the fact that on most campuses, fraternities are allowed to have alcohol but sororities remain dry.

On April 4, 2011, the Department of Justice delivered what was known as the Dear Colleague Letter (DCL) to colleges and universities. It was an exhaustively detailed letter with a lengthy set of guidelines on how to respond to and adjudicate all forms of sexual violence. It announced that failure to meet the standards set forth in the DCL would be a violation under Title IX. The initial reaction to the DCL was tepid and unnoticeable on most campuses. However, in the aftermath of a few high-profile cases and the releases of the documentary *The Hunting Ground* and the book *Missoula: Rape and the Justice System in a College Town* by John Krakauer, both in 2015, more than three thousand investigations were opened by the Department of Education's Office for Civil Rights. While the lever of Title IX is primarily legalese and largely investigatory and punitive, it has also sparked the necessary steps to accelerate effective conversations about violence prevention.

What has emerged is a cottage industry of prevention programs, old and new, that are backed by an influx of resources and support from national initiatives such as It's On Us, which originated in the Obama White House. Stakeholders throughout higher education are responding to an imperative issue that has existed since 1840, the year Catherine Brewer became the first woman to graduate with a bachelor's degree from Wesleyan College in Macon, Georgia. The women who have who followed her legacy have exposed the sexism and misogyny on campuses and continue to force a more transparent conversation.

BLUE LIGHTS ON CAMPUS

As a young black football player who attended a predominantly white college, my presence was conspicuous. I was afforded a privileged education along with the power of my affiliation with one of the most high-profile entities on campus—football. Despite that privilege, my identity as a black man was like having an alter ego, keeping me on guard for discrimination and bias in every aspect of my life on campus. While safety was not a concern, I was vulnerable to experiencing racism in many other forms. It was, by no means, the front lines of violent racism and discrimination, but the threat always lay just below the surface. I knew that as much as my notoriety as an athlete was an identity that gave me a discernible privilege, my predominant and inextricable identity was as a black man. This experience exposed me to the fluidity of privilege.

When I first started my engagement work on college campuses, I tried to compare the experiences of women to my own. I realized that despite my concern that I would face prejudice and discrimination, in a physical sense, I was in fact very safe. I could not say the same for my female counterparts, black, white, and brown, and I grew acutely aware of those measures in place to make them feel safe, providing the same false sense of security (which included learning about "the list" for college women).

Prior to the DCL, most schools acknowledged a small number of sexual assaults—to state that none occurred would obviously be disingenuous. But to offer actual and real statistics, numbers of reports, or known incidents would alarm the parents of daughters, the demographic that has become their best customers. In spite of all efforts to downplay the risk of danger, the actions taken and resources in place on campuses depicted a much different reality. Again, seeking a comparative perspective, I imagined a parallel situation where my parents were informed by my school that there were only a few reported incidents of violence and racism in the past year *but* the school's student handbook featured a section detailing the following tips for me and other black men on how to be safe on campus:

- *Instructions on how to dress in shared spaces with white students.*
- *Keep doors locked, especially after hours.*
- *Use the "buddy system," traveling together with other black students when you go out.*

I also imagined the safety resources promoted in the handbook:

- *White student volunteers are available to walk you across campus.*

- *Nighttime vans available to shuttle you to and from academic buildings and the library.*
- *In the event of attack, off-campus crisis centers and hotlines with trained experts are standing by.*

Lastly, in my imagination, if I ever felt imminently threatened, the school strategically placed emergency phone stations throughout campus, each clearly marked by a blue light, which provided a direct link to the campus safety office.

Now, I understand the risk my predecessors endured as African American students on predominantly white college campuses in the early days of integration. They did not have such safeguards in place that ensured their safety, yet the students enrolled anyway, risking serious hardship to make historic change. Still, in my first year of college in 1983, the scenario above would have been outrageous. How could my parents have felt comfortable leaving me at school—even if I was the quarterback of the football team?

What I presented earlier are the guidelines and services in place *today* on college campuses to address the threat of men's violence against women. They serve as an admission of a problem that the rhetoric of "a few reported incidents in the past year" tries to diminish. Why would so many guidelines and services be in place if only a few students per year were reporting a problem? They are all extensions of "the list," and they perpetuate the paradigm that women should be blamed for their victimization.

This is also, once again, a flawed strategy of "prevention" that is more accurately defined as "risk reduction." Installing systems to mitigate legal exposure is *not* true prevention. That requires eliminating the source of the problem. On the surface, college campuses are not hostile places for women. But when you move beyond the brochures and colleges' stated ideals, what women experience in higher education is not dissimilar from the sexism, misogyny, and unbridled patriarchy they encounter off campus. What is more blatant is the impunity with which these dynamics are played out, the ways in which men are relatively unchecked in their interactions with women. Warning women and teaching them how to survive in this setting, while doing nothing to teach men how to respectfully engage with them, inevitably fosters destructive behaviors in both groups. Neither is exposed to any real conversations about how to navigate intimacy or relationships before they arrive on campus. Both are influenced by the predominant and often grotesque interpretations of their respective gender peer cultures that reflect and perpetuate traditional expectations but with a generational expression. In other words, narrowly defined and strictly held gender rules, social traditions, and hierarchies that are as patriarchal and sexist as they are provincial, and they persist. Therefore, the sexually predatory behavior of college men continues uninterrupted.

THE SCRIPT

As discussed, college men often exhibit some of the most socially egregious, appalling, and dangerous behavior. Their behavior is a manifestation of years of socialization (the promise and performance of the mandate of masculinity), unleashed in an unsupervised postadolescent playground designed for independence and growth. Yet the mandate of masculinity does not require growth but endurance of performing "what not to be." So, they arrive on campus with little experience negotiating intimate relationships and with a lack of understanding of themselves as emotional and gendered people.

To explain why college men engage in sexually predatory

behavior, we often blame the copious amounts of alcohol that flood the campus environment. In actuality, alcohol only serves the purpose of lowering men's inhibitions; it reveals their attitudes and expectations more than it causes them. I believe their impulses are governed more by what informs "the heat of the moment," which I referred to in a sports context in Chapter Three and will explore more fully in Chapter Eight. In the heat of the moment, we react on the basis of what we've been taught and how we've been conditioned. And when parents and other adults fail to talk honestly about sexual intimacy with young people, peer culture does the teaching and conditioning for them. It provides the missing script, with language drawn from a common gendered experience to which everyone must strictly conform.

To illustrate the expectations and pressures on college men and the disturbing perspective from which many operate—both with each other and with women—I created a scenario. Featuring an interaction between two college teammates and a fictional version of me, it goes like this . . .

> *After a good workout with George and Mike, we go to a local restaurant and bar just off campus for a burger. As night falls and the place fills up, I see a woman across the room (and I give every indication that I find her very attractive). I tell George that I'm going over to talk with her. I spend the next forty-five minutes talking to her. Then I tell Mike that I am just going to walk her to her car. But I don't come back.*
>
> *The next day, when I see George and Mike in the locker room, what do they ask?*

The first time I used that scenario was in a general campus-wide presentation at a small New England college. I knew where I wanted to take the discussion and I knew the general response that the scenario would elicit. Then, in a full room that included administrators and faculty, a young female student gave a knee-jerk response, shouting, "Did ya hit it?" Three thoughts immediately rushed my brain: I was not expecting a response from a *female* student (especially not *that* response); I was impressed that she felt safe and free enough to be that explicit; and I was excited and filled with gratitude for her permission to delve deeper. For that, I was ready!

She expressed a graphic truth and summarily exposed how boys and men encourage and enforce the objectification and sexual dehumanization of women. Her instant comeback shed light on the "hookup culture" so prevalent on college campuses, its expectations of sexual intimacy, and the universally known ways in which we all talk about intimacy in violent and emotionally detached ways. What was disheartening was the profound irony that *she* articulated the sentiment. As a woman, she recognized she was the "it," the *thing* that got "hit."

In almost every instance of narrating the scenario, when I mention the length of time that I talked with the woman, students laugh at me, suggesting that forty-five minutes is a very long time to be "talking." Their laughter is significant because it demonstrates one of the primary reasons I created the scenario—to expose the problems associated with the distorted assumption that I "hooked up" with the woman. Not only did they understand that my friends expected me to hook up, but in their eyes, forty-five minutes was an exorbitant length of time to negotiate a casual sexual encounter. This thinking is poisonous in so many ways. I remind students that in all other endeavors (academics, sports), we make good decisions on the basis of comprehensive and reliable information that often takes a great deal of time to obtain, test, and prove. I ask, "How can I possibly be making a good decision about being intimate with that woman after a forty-five-minute exchange in a bar?"

When I was in college, not a day went by that if I was seen talking to a female student, a teammate would ask or imply, "You hittin' that?" No matter the setting or circumstance, even if it was obvious that there was no connection between me and a nearby woman, I was still offered an opportunity to declare myself "in the hunt." The question plays an essential role in maintaining the mandate and performance of masculinity. It's a way for men to monitor the others in their circle and ensure they remain in a position of perpetual domination and hunt for women. To do otherwise would be a betrayal of patriarchal privilege.

The exchange that follows that question is meaningful as well: anyone's claim that they are not engaged "in the hunt" is met with a sharp rebuke, such as, "What's *wrong* with you?" "Are you scared?" "Are you gay?" Immediately, one's masculine bona fides are questioned, triggering a barrage of overt sexist, misogynistic, and homophobic attacks.

The sad reality of this performance is that it's less about actual behavior with a woman and more about demonstrating adherence to the mandate in the form of male bonding. I can recall with embarrassment the times when, instead of truthfully denying that I was "chasing" or actually intimate with a woman, I simply smiled and said, "Yeah, you know me," keeping the illusion alive to maintain my masculine credibility. I was, in fact, only protecting an immature and insecure form of masculinity. Moreover, I was putting that woman at risk (of reputation and safety) by allowing my friends to believe that she was intimate with a man she didn't even know.

The language and tone that many men use to talk about sex

illustrate a violent and emotionally detached understanding of sexual intimacy, one that eviscerates the physical and emotional connection that is the very essence of an intimate relationship.

Did you hit IT?
Did you get SOME?
Did you get a PIECE of THAT?

Referring to a woman with any of these expressions is the truest and most insidious form of objectification: they are reduced to ornamental props in the performance of masculinity. At one of the most significant moments of human encounter, where the experience is by definition mutual, such language perverts the moment and makes it anything but. Boys and men bond around this language. It is rooted in a dangerously insecure view of masculinity in which the act of sex is seen more as something done *to* a woman and less as a loving, shared experience *with* a woman.

FIRST WE DEHUMANIZE OURSELVES

The above scenario and the expectations of the characters in it demonstrate how the devaluing of women, part of the performance of masculinity, serves to achieve a distorted and transactional sexual experience that also fulfills the mandate of masculinity. We have been socialized to believe that this is the accomplishment. As with my fight with Sidney, the actual performance is less important than how it's represented among our peers. In other words, it is not about pleasing one's partner but proving to other men the prowess to achieve the opportunity.

Devaluing and objectifying a woman distinguishes her from other women whom we associate with love and respect— grandmothers, mothers, sisters, and daughters. Once that happens, men feel they can treat that woman with disrespect, contempt, and even violence. It allows men to dissociate themselves as well, to *not* see themselves as a son, brother, or father. We must disassociate ourselves from the natural urge to relinquish control and be vulnerable to another person for whom we have feelings and affection—our humanity.

The process of dehumanizing women further cements the narrow way in which we as men understand our own humanity, which means we also become dehumanized. To view women as objects that we "do something to" sexually, we must first view ourselves as emotionally incompetent "things" incapable of embracing the qualities of women that make them and us human. We must first dehumanize and objectify ourselves; unworthy of and expelling all expectations of emotional fulfillment and connection.

This is a narrative that gets told many ways throughout a boy's life: his emotions and intimate care are not necessary for his successful navigation of life. This dynamic is readily and consistently obvious in so many of our relationships with women. This further illustrates the blind spot of masculinity that keeps men from wholeness and fulfillment.

This is the critical intersection between men's violence against women and narrow masculinity. Just as the lives of women and men are inextricable, so too are these issues. Whether they want to or not, women represent the vulnerability and empathy that men spend a lifetime beating out of themselves and each other. Yet relationships with women force us to reveal those qualities. While the results are positive when this occurs in loving, respectful relationships, in the absence of those relationships, it can be tragic.

While there has been some progress in confronting the dangerous messages that sustain the myth of masculinity and the paradigm of men's dominance over women, overall we remain reluctant to engage in honest dialogue, especially if it threatens privilege or the perception of privilege that comes with ignoring our human vulnerabilities. Avoiding that urgent conversation means we will be confronted with hard truths that hit much closer to home than we want to consider.

 *Traditions of Silence*

EMANUELLE IN BANGKOK

My mother always took us to the Lynbrook theater when the really big movies came out. It was close to the schools where she worked as a nurse and where my siblings and I attended grade school. Across the street was Vincent's Pizzeria, which made that area a popular destination for families. We saw everything from the animated *Aristocats* and *Jaws* to *The Pink Panther* and *Ben*, the film about a boy and his army of rats.

It was also the place where I saw pornography for the first time. I was twelve years old.

The theater was not some seedy venue in a red-light district. It was familiar to me, and on that bright, sunny afternoon, the idea of pornography only felt slightly deviant. This was also primarily because I didn't know exactly what pornography was or what I would be seeing that afternoon.

Reggie Williams, the older brother of my best friend Dave, told us that *Emanuelle in Bangkok* was playing and if we could get there, we could get in. Dave was two years older than me, and Reggie, who served in the military, was several years older than Dave. The large difference in their ages made their relationship quite different than what I had with my brothers. Reggie was a bridge to a world that I was told I was not ready for and was too young to understand. He also represented the mandate of masculinity that insisted that knowing about girls and sex is central to what made you a "real man." And even though I had no idea what they were actually talking about when they talked about girls and sex, I always acted as if I did. I can remember, one afternoon, looking at a magazine of naked women, getting an erection, and actually saying out loud, "What do I do now?" We laughed and it became a long-standing joke between us, but I was serious.

At that age, *looking* at naked women in a magazine was about all I could handle. It was what we did at that stage of the performance, and it validated my masculinity, making me one of the guys. When Reggie brought up the idea of going to see the movie, it felt more like a command than a suggestion. And since I carried on like I knew about sex, I had to take the lie one step further.

I remember my fear as we approached the theater. I felt alone. I couldn't share my anxiety with Dave and, thinking ahead to when I'd get home, I certainly couldn't discuss the experience with anyone there, not even my brothers. I also felt like I had no choice. This was a rite of passage. So we walked . . . and I remained silent.

After the movie, as we headed home, I learned that Dave had never seen porn either. But he didn't show any of the anxiety I had. (Maybe I didn't show it either—that thought was comforting.) I figured he was better at masking his lack of experience than I was; after all, he had learned enough from Reggie to talk a good game. Nevertheless, we acted as if we both knew what it was all about. I was certainly not going to ask any questions that would indicate how naive I actually was and that I had no idea what I'd just witnessed. Aside from some nervous laughter, the only lasting discussion was about the music. For me, it was like the music in all horror films, serving as a warning—time to look away to avoid the nightmares that were sure to follow.

The moving images we saw on the screen that day complemented the still images that, until that moment, were our first and only exposure to women in any sexual context. Since we had no real-life experiences as a point of comparison, the film presented us a dangerously misleading reality. While what we saw on the screen that day may have been pornography, to us it was sex, intimacy, and love. The "sex" we witnessed paralleled how we were coming to understand ourselves as boys: in a way that was emotionally detached. And while we were exposed to graphic sexual behavior, it was depicted without any of the emotional accountability that should exist between intimate partners.

The next day, Reggie congratulated Dave and me as if we had graduated to a new level of education. I acted as though the whole experience was just another day. Yet despite my cool disposition, I knew it was a big deal. It had validated our masculinity.

SEARCHING FOR THE TRUTH . . . ABOUT ME

I was twelve years old, exploring my independence and seeking validation of my masculine identity from the culture of boys and men around me. To push the boundaries of that exploration meant living beyond the confines of my immediate family, learning about those things that were discussed in hushed tones at home, if at all. There was no topic more cryptic and intriguing than sex. In fact, any reference to it began and ended with "you're not ready" and "when you get older." That made it more provocative and made me eager to discover its secret. So in the absence of the knowledge and wisdom of the adults in my life, I explored.

This episode reminds me of how lost, ignorant, and naive I once was. It also brings back memories of the awkward transition from not being interested in girls to the mandate of needing to know what they, and sex, were all about. At that time of my life, I was also beginning to excel as an athlete, which made for an ironic situation. The development of my physicality and athletic skills received acute attention from the adults in my life. But my development as a man—the mastery of my emotional toolbox and ideas of intimacy, sexuality, and maturity—was left to happenstance.

Most of us have had a Dave or Reggie in our life, especially in our youth—a close friend who advanced our experiences beyond the capacity or the willingness of our immediate circle of influence. Reggie was also a constant reminder and symbol of the performance of masculinity when it came to girls and sex: *Have sex, have it often, and be cool about it.* The funny thing was, it was as if he had all the answers about a subject I hadn't realized I had to know . . . until I realized I *had* to know.

Walking to Lynbrook to see *Emanuelle* was evidence of how far I was willing to go to satisfy my curiosity. What little I learned at the theater that afternoon was enough to support stories I had heard, no matter how shallow or inaccurate, as well as fill gaps left empty by the silence from the adults in my life. I had been given a visual image—and seeing is believing. The moans, smiles, and insatiable pursuit of the next encounter, especially by Emanuelle herself, substantiated Reggie's interpretation of sex. Everyone seemed to be enjoying themselves in the film. And the men were in charge, just as Reggie told us they should be. The truth was, I learned very little from Reggie beyond the expectation that I needed to know and embrace a specific attitude of emotionally detached male dominance. I actually had very little interaction with Reggie. My reference to him here is a euphemism for the pressure I was experiencing at the time from the world around me about the expectations of masculinity.

It's important to note the fundamental importance of the "sex narrative" to the performance of masculinity. There is no greater or more acute requirement of the performance than the challenge to remain emotionally distant and invulnerable. This is especially true with regard to that which we covet most, true love and physical intimacy. At best, men in the sex narrative demonstrate an emotionally cool distance and even indifference. At worst is what we witness in most pornography: complete disregard for the female partner while male actors perform total dominance and control, and even violence.

For all intents and purposes, this was my experience with the "streets," a term that refers to any place where we learned the things that our parents were reluctant or incapable of speaking about forthrightly and honestly. Nearly all children learn the lessons of the streets; they become reality in the absence of more informed and experienced perspectives provided by trusted adults.

Most parents worry about the influence of the streets because they don't want their children to get bad messages or the "wrong idea." They know how inaccurate the stories from the streets can be and don't want their children misled as they once were. Yet they often do nothing to provide good messages and positive ideas and understanding. Instead, they function like a hypervigilant hockey goalie attempting to block out the barrage of sexual messages, images, jokes, and innuendos that inundate the lives of young people.

In my youth, the streets were a physical location—a basement, backyard, the town park, or literally a street corner. For me, it was mostly the town park. The "streets" were free of supervision, though not free of the adult men who sought their obscurity for their nefarious behavior. Although not a dangerous environment, it wasn't one my parents preferred. But they were attentive, and by controlling when we were out of the house, they limited the negative influences on us.

Things have changed since those days. Today, in many ways, "the streets" is a figurative term. The detrimental influences that reach beyond parental control are not confined to a physical location or limited by any group or community. It is an amorphous space enabled by mobile technology and Internet access. "The streets" are held in the palm of a child's hand, accessible twenty four hours a day.

Access and exposure to information has increased, while the level of adults' engagement with children remains relatively the same when it comes to those topics that we have all been raised *not* to talk about—especially sex. In my early days of working with young students, I recognized and understood parents' apprehension to take on difficult topics. But when I started working with college students, it quickly became evident that the conversations usually never happened at all.

GRAPHIC, HONEST, AND SUSTAINED

When I speak to a group of college students, I often take a poll: "Raise your hand if your parent, grandparent, or whoever raised you, supported you, and helped get you this far in life also gave you a graphic, honest, and sustained conversation about your bodies, intimacy, and sexual behavior."

When I initially began taking the poll back in 1999, on a regular basis no more than 2 percent of the room raised their hands. Today, the response remains relatively the same, with never more than 5 percent of hands affirming they had an honest and ongoing dialogue about sexual behavior. It's an astonishing piece of data that is hard to reconcile with what I generally assume of these students, which is that before entering college, they receive a modicum of sound guidance to help them generally make good life decisions. No matter that background, this seems an essential requirement for them earning a place in higher education.

For the 95 percent who don't raise their hands, I ask a follow-up question: "If you didn't get the information from your parents, where did you get it?"

I receive several answers: "older siblings," "friends," "sex education class." But overwhelmingly, "media" is cited as the greatest source of information. As I will explore in the next chapter, the ubiquitous presence of media in our lives provides an infinite source of both information on and interpretations of sexual behavior (as well as masculinity).

Yet despite the pervasive nature of media, parents and other adult figures can still play the most influential role in how children grow to understand relationships, intimacy, and themselves—as long as they actively play that role. If they remain silent, they transfer that role to other insidious influences.

The battle to shield young people from these influences is more difficult than ever. The reality is that many parents have simply not kept pace; they have essentially capitulated to other adults who want to control the thoughts and behaviors of children and their understanding of sexuality. Those "other adults" are often advertising agencies and entertainment companies that use sex and sexual imagery to shock or stimulate to profit financially. They may also be sexual predators who take advantage of the naivete of their targets.

It is a sad irony that while most children are conceived in the beauty of intimate and vulnerable love, their understanding of their conception is often first shaped by what is presented to them through emotionally detached and often violently sexist pornography. Why are two people who conceived a child reluctant to share the process of conception with that same child?

Why do we, as a society, keep the most intimate and important moments of human life a secret?

We tell children to wait until they are old enough, but when is that exactly? Part of the problem is that it's often the adults, not the children, who are uncomfortable having an open and honest discussion. Sometimes they get caught up in the moral dimension of the issue. They remain inert as they struggle to reconcile their own views on sex and what is appropriate with how they themselves were raised. Meanwhile, children remain in the dark regarding the basic facts about their own bodies.

Remember the "Birds and the Bees" talk? I never heard it myself, so I don't know what that story was or how it was supposed to explain human intimacy. The Wikipedia entry on "The Birds and the Bees" explains it as "the metaphorical story sometimes told to children in an attempt to explain the mechanics and good consequences of sexual intercourse through reference to easily observed natural events." Now, I observed a lot of birds and bees when I was a boy. I saw nothing in their behavior that prepared me for *Emanuelle*. The film's portrayal of sex and intimacy was much more aligned with the story told by Reggie and *Playboy*.

CYCLE OF SILENCE

My mother and father shared a pragmatic attitude, which made them good at dealing with life's harsh truths. In most things we discussed, there was brutal honesty and respectful, open discussion. However, when it came to sex, they did not speak a word.

None of us expected any talks about intimacy from my father, and his silence transferred power to other people and other sources of information. My mother, like most moms, was loving, nurturing, and empathic. That was also in keeping with her profession as a registered nurse. Her empathy and caring served as a counterweight to my dad's stoicism. Through her abundant patience, she eased our fears and showed that we could be safe in the world. She was awesome when it came to dealing with everyday scrapes and bruises, her bedside manner was gentle and reassuring, and we were certain no ailment would go untreated. Yet as with my dad, she didn't talk to me about sex, intimacy, or the changes occurring with our bodies.

My mother was a nurse in elementary and middle schools. When I asked her if she talked about the subject with any of my siblings, reluctantly she admitted she had not. But she did recall the story of a boy who came to her to ask about a bodily change he was experiencing. She was surprised the student came to her because it was a sensitive issue. Nevertheless, her advice to him was that the changes were normal and that he had nothing to worry about. I'm sure she felt more comfortable talking with her own children, but since we never brought those sensitive matters to her, there was no occasion to discuss them. When I asked if her parents had ever had "the talk" with her, her response was curt: "Absolutely NOT!"

That abrupt response is what you expect when asking most adults if they talked with *their* parents about sex. The uneasiness about this issue is painfully clear. It's likely they never got the talk, so why should they know how or when to give it? This is how the sad cycle of silence is perpetuated and becomes as entrenched as any other tradition.

Some parents may think, *Since I never got the talk, let them learn like I did.* Others simply don't know how to handle the subject. If you never learned that sex and your own body are okay subjects to discuss, how would you ever develop the skills to approach the topics openly and tactfully when talking with your own children? While this is a real dilemma for parents, for children it can be an extremely confusing, awkward, and even dangerous time. Parents need to understand that children are not coming from a deviant place or with salacious intentions. The topics and questions may be beyond the comfort zone of parents, but we must remain open to our children's curiosity and not judge their questions. This may be the most difficult challenge of parenting, but it's also where meaningful conversations can and must begin.

SCARE TACTICS DON'T WORK

In the 1980s, when I began my career working with young people on issues of alcohol and other drugs, I served as a proxy voice for adults who had either acquiesced or were ill-equipped to speak honestly with their children. At least that's how I viewed my role, since I was essentially saying the same things as the adults in their lives. But young people witnessed the unhealthy behavior of those adults and therefore could see past the prevention rhetoric. I often felt that my primary function was to support the general hypocrisy and inability of adults to speak honestly; the message was, "Do as Don says, not as I do."

When I began the work of addressing men's violence against women, I again encountered prevention language and scare tactics regarding the topic we are most reluctant to discuss—sex. In fact, it was core to the fundamental message, and unfortunately it largely remains that way today. We tell young people, "Sex is dirty and immoral; it will cause unwanted pregnancies that will ruin your life and result in all manners and forms of disease." And almost in the same breath, we tell them to "save it for that one special person, the one you love."

I believe the language of fear is just as unhealthy. When I spoke about issues of drugs and alcohol, all I could offer was prevention language and scare tactics that supported some larger campaign to stop or prevent certain behavior. I was never comfortable with that approach. Moreover, the conversation about sexual behavior and violence is more nuanced; the continuum on which sexual behavior is learned is fluid, alluring, and as subtle as it is powerful. Scare tactics and prevention language do not change or influence behavior; if they did, we would see examples of them in sports and education, with coaches showing teams how "not to lose" and teachers showing students how "not to fail." This isn't standard in these fields; both are grounded in the sequential process of learning how to master skills, understanding how things work, and developing positive attitudes and habits that allow for positive outcomes to be repeated. Likewise, any conversation around social behavior must include those same principles.

Another problem with the rhetoric about fear is that we tell horror stories that rarely materialize. I observed this phenomenon regarding alcohol. Kids witness relatively harmless drinking at a far greater rate than they do drinking with tragic outcomes; consequently, the warnings they hear from adults don't match the reality before their eyes. And when young people see adults using and celebrating drug and alcohol use, the message becomes further compromised.

Young people will see the hollowness of adults' warnings about alcohol and drug use. Likewise, when they learn about or engage in sex and it doesn't result in pregnancy or disease, the fear invoked by those warnings about sex begins to wane in favor of the fleeting pleasure it provides.

GOING BEYOND THE TALK

In reality, there is no easy way to talk to children about sex. One solitary "talk" is not the answer. We must cultivate a diligent way of life that normalizes the conversation. The "talk" must actually be an ongoing conversation with children, and it can't be based in fear or judgment. We must do more than just provide information; we must also process children's feelings and expectations as well as our own. There may be right or wrong behaviors, but there are no right or wrong questions. Parents need to put their hopes of an "end goal" aside to allow children to fully process and understand a complex aspect of our humanity.

Ultimately, the decisions young people make are all their own. Parents and other adults can only strive to give children accurate and comprehensive information so they can make good decisions. The stories parents tell can't have holes or be filled with scare tactics that don't match what children have observed or will observe; otherwise the message will be compromised and children will have a reason to question this type of authority.

Children will be led into secretive behavior while they begin to *think* they understand. Their defenses will increase around adults because adults have taken the hard line of intolerance and fear. Communication can then break down—parents stop listening to children and the conversation becomes a one-way diatribe. Children will hide their discoveries of the world, as well as their attitudes and behaviors.

Children may also hide their knowledge of certain things out of a desire to *protect* adults. If adults dwell too much on the dangers of the world, children may begin to believe the adults are simply afraid and ought to be shielded. With each passing generation children are exposed to a broader, less restrictive lens on the world. Some children may assume that adults warn them because they (adults) can't handle the reality of the changing world. In other cases, adults are aware of what children are going through but lack the tools and experiences to talk honestly with them, so they resort to bribery, cajoling, and harsh zero-tolerance policies. Many more will simply accept the fact that their children are "going through a phase" that they will outgrow like a pair of sneakers. But unlike those discarded sneakers, phases have a cumulative effect and can be foundational to a person's development. Unless inaccurate and unhealthy beliefs are confronted, they can become more entrenched and the basis for toxic and destructive learned behaviors.

All of these factors place parents in a difficult position, but disregarding them can lead to serious incidents involving young people. In the aftermath, parents are in the even more difficult position of trying to explain why something terrible occurred in the first place. The most effective approach parents can take is to engage with children in a proactive, ongoing conversation that is honest, fosters two-way communication, and allows children space to fully process information. For boys, this is a pivotal time, as it is also the time when the emotional mask of masculinity hardens, and with it diminishing opportunities for meaningful conversation.

WHEN PERCEPTION BECOMES REALITY

When you examine *how* boys are learning, *what* they are learning becomes easier to comprehend. So many of their attitudes and beliefs are learned in unstructured ways. And since so many boys share the same inaccurate beliefs, with no credible source to disprove them, rumors and inaccuracies become true.

This dynamic applies to how boys' beliefs about gender and sexuality are formed. Because their perception becomes reality, they act out and legitimize misconceptions and fantasies, confident that they are acting appropriately. Similar to how the pornography of *Emanuelle* was conflated with "lovemaking," boys form other dangerous and sexist assumptions about relationships with girls. We now talk of "affirmative consent," because "no means no" was not deliberate enough and men continue to express expectations of intimacy if he pays for a meal or if she has been intimate in the past.

These misconceptions also reduce relationships and intimacy to "games," positioning girls and women as opposing figures, not partners. Intimate advancements are not viewed as an expression of mutual desire or agreed-upon exploration but a benchmark, an achieved level in the performance of masculinity. There are also times when the dangerous "lessons" from the streets are sanctioned by adults and essentially handed to children. Though dressed up as innocent fun, these lessons can perpetuate disturbing attitudes and beliefs. I remember the rumor of Spanish fly, a substance you put in a girl's drink that would make her uncontrollably promiscuous. The first time I heard of it was listening to a comedy album by Bill Cosby. He talked about being thirteen, standing on the corner with all the boys, talking about Crazy Mary, the girl in his neighborhood who was the target of the Spanish fly assault. But his story went further than being a funny routine—it revealed a common desire among many boys and men to treat a girl or woman in this disgraceful manner.

Cosby was the comedian we were allowed to listen to because he didn't curse or tell explicit jokes. He was wholesome, family-friendly fun. Sadly, and horrifically, Cosby was found guilty of three counts of aggravated indecent assault in 2018. He employed a method similar to what he described in his routine, using illegal drugs on women to render them helpless to his sexual assaults. He made the concept of Spanish fly humorous; even if we didn't fully understand then, we did learn at least that he was fine with manipulating a woman for his pleasure, and that this was accepted comedy from adults.

Although Cosby has been called a monster, customs such as "ladies' night" at bars share troubling similarities with his tactics. As a drug, alcohol lowers inhibition and is the most commonly used substance for men to facilitate the manipulation and sexual assault of women. While certain drugs (Rohypnol or GHB) are vilified as "date-rape drugs," alcohol is overwhelmingly the most commonly used drug to cloud a woman's judgment and disable her ability to deploy the preventive strategies of "the list."

Legally, in most states, intoxication cannot be used as a defense in cases of rape and sexual assault. This protects both men and women, although we generally only consider this a protection for women. Such laws are written based on what we know from history and experience, and also influence how we understand the impact of alcohol on sexual "consent." Still we see promotions such as ladies' nights, which in my opinion should be illegal. The purpose of providing alcohol for free or at a reduced cost to women is to attract women to a bar, but it also encourages unrestrained consumption. Bar owners do this knowing men will follow behind, in search of large crowds of intoxicated women. But feeling they must "catch up" to their counterparts, men drink aggressively, allowing the bar owner to recoup the loss from comping drinks to women. The strategy makes for a lucrative evening for the bar owner but potentially a dangerous one for both women and men.

The situations that I've described here that involve illegal behavior, or are at least rooted in nefarious intent, can feel much like my trip to see *Emanuelle*—sanctioned by peers and taking place in a safe, familiar environment. Participants might feel only slightly deviant because they lack a true apprehension of what's going on. College men, in particular, are vulnerable to this scenario. In an environment free of many restraints and that presumably offers them license to demonstrate their learned version of sexual intimacy, these men can become both perpetrator and victim. They grasp the expectation of their performance, but not the reality of their behavior . . . or its legal implications. Unfortunately, too often it is only in the aftermath of a sexual assault involving alcohol that we finally engage men in a sober conversation about sexual behavior and intimacy. But this is also when men become defensive, blaming women or alcohol as a way to deny their own culpability.

THE TALK IS TOO LATE

The one topic we all have in common is the most difficult to discuss. Why is any public discussion of sexual behavior immediately considered to be inappropriate, racy, or deviant? And what is the impact on our children's understanding of sex and intimacy when it's exclusively used with base and dirty language, or to shock or degrade? What is the impact of this approach on young people trying to develop healthy understandings and behaviors? There is also the problem of "prevention language," which I mentioned earlier. Because of the focus on the negative consequences of irresponsible sexual behavior, open discussion of sexual behavior frequently comes in the form of warnings. Even when we do choose to discuss an issue, there remain tremendous flaws in the ways they are addressed. We often choose to address *symptoms* of the problem, such as alcohol, or simply remain silent.

For the record, I'm not endorsing a curriculum that teaches the use of contraception and "safe sex." My view is much more radical and offensive. I think we need to be telling kids about their bodies so they can understand themselves as sexual beings. The binary choice we've made of telling them to have safe sex or ignoring it completely is not the answer. The more information they receive, the better decisions they can and will make.

During the 1980s, a concerted social movement to address drunk driving introduced the idea of a "designated driver." Today, the makers of alcoholic beverages continue to preach the need to designate a driver. While one person chooses not to drink, the passengers are afforded unbridled permission to drink to excess. While the number of drunk drivers on the road may have been reduced, the problem of alcoholism and the litany of other alcohol-related problems continue. Similarly, the answer to dealing with teen pregnancy and STIs is not condoms and/or abstinence. To be absolutely certain, abstinence is the only true way to prevent the onslaught of problems associated with sexual behavior; however, I do not think it's realistic in our culture. We cannot expect our children to practice abstinence and allow the advertising and entertainment industries to continue to use hypersexualized images, innuendoes, and themes without bearing some responsibility in this discussion.

READY OR NOT . . .

At a dinner party recently, I overheard a friend share a story about how she happened upon her five-year-old son playing with his erection. It was the first time she "caught him in the act." She was talking with a group of friends, all of whom were young moms. Being within earshot, I leaned in, curious to hear their discussion. They all knew her son and I sensed their empathy, as she was describing a boy who had clearly just discovered something of which he had very little understanding. She went on to say how she tried to ignore it so he would not be embarrassed. Doing my best not to get clinical, I suggested that next time, she give him a sippy cup of juice and ask him if he was having fun with his new "activity." Walking the line between friend and educator, I left it at that. But stepping away I thought, *He has nothing to be embarrassed about. He is a child who was innocently learning about his own body. She was projecting her "shame" on him.*

Moments later, I came across the boy's dad. He is a close friend and I could not resist broaching the subject. With a smile, I said, "Hey, I heard little Mike got his first hard-on." A proud smile came upon my friend's face as he proclaimed, "Yeah, that's my boy." We shared a sophomoric high five and exchanged a few jokes exaggerating the size of his genitalia—the thing men do to laugh through our insecurities. It was a good laugh until I asked what he said to little Mike. He became austere and said, "He's not ready for that." My demeanor became equally as stern, as I realized I had to step over the prohibitive line of friend and speak as an educator. I told him little Mike may not be ready for the conversation about *why* his penis gets erect, but he was certainly ready to hear that an erect penis is normal and okay. And it's critically important that he hear that from his dad.

Both parents responded to an innocent moment with conditioned, narrow thinking about the physical nature of humans and the way in which boys and men are taught to understand themselves sexually. The mother was embarrassed for her son and the father failed to recognize and seize the opportunity to teach his boy a healthy lesson about his body. Both parents missed a chance to establish a fundamental level of communication and start a sustained conversation that would strengthen their son's self-esteem as well as their relationship with him.

The fact is, his body was responding to something; he should understand that and know that it is perfectly normal. Clearly, a five-year-old is probably not ready to talk about reproduction. But he is ready to understand how his body works. However, many adults are so bound by a shame tracing back to how they were socialized to understand their own bodies that they are unable to give their children the information they need. Their continued silence limits boys' ability to see themselves as beautiful beings worthy of physical love.

If nothing is said, and there is no explanation given, the boy's penis will seem to be responding independent of his control. Little Mike's erection becomes the thing that happens to his body, not a natural function of it. It marks the beginning of the notion of the "little head" that seemingly has a mind of its own, and the beginning of the emotional disconnect a boy will have with his body. Later he will learn to understand that sexual acts are what he does *to* girls and that he carries them out with the object that is his body, devoid of any emotional engagement and accountability. The violent language he uses to describe sex ("hit it," "bang it," "smash") only makes sense if he sees himself as the object—that tool used to hit, bang, or smash.

You may say that I am making too much of a young boy innocently playing with his erect penis. But this is merely one part of a much broader socializing process. How a boy understands and loves his own body is the measure by which he can and will extend love and care to another. Understanding and openly talking about this aspect of human sexuality has been one of those issues men have avoided. In 1994, when Surgeon General Joycelyn Elders suggested that the subject of masturbation should be covered as part of comprehensive sex education for elementary school children, she was forced by President Bill Clinton to resign amid pressure from his administration. Elder was not encouraging debauchery but advocating for healthy sexual behavior. In response, the largely male Congress literally made a federal case out of masturbation.

A responsible adult culture should always try to make the world better for the next generation. We cannot expect this to happen by withholding information and being silent, especially about the essential things that make us human. We can't have an intelligent conversation about sexual violence until we're ready to acknowledge that we are sexual beings who need and crave physical affection.

THE PARENT DILEMMA

When a friend told me her ten-year-old son and his friends searched the word "sex" on an iPad, my first thought was, *They're two years younger than I was when my curiosity took me a few miles away on foot*. Her son and his friends are good boys and their curiosity was no different than mine. But unlike my trek to the theater, these boys were in the same room where their parents lulled them to sleep reading *Goodnight Moon*. And, when they did an Internet search for "sex," the Italian sexploitation/drama film *Emanuelle in Bangkok* is surely not what they found. The pornography is commercial, hard-core, and quite disturbing. Certainly, the boys knew that what they were doing would not meet the approval of their parents. They understood the risk of being caught but their curiosity and desire for truth was more compelling.

Naturally, my friend was quite upset to imagine her son being exposed to such pornography. However, what was more upsetting was the idea that he didn't feel comfortable talking with her. As she processed this with her son, she learned that the other boys had been punished by their parents; their devices had been taken away and limits were placed on their time with technology. This, I thought, was the more predictable and likely response, and the most troubling.

This response creates shame in the boy and shuts down any possibility of conversations in the immediate future, if not forever, about what he is feeling, concerned with, thinking about, or, more urgently, experiencing. Second, it suggests he has done something wrong and that his curiosity is dirty and shameful, and that sex is inherently bad. Ironically, those same parents,

186 ♦ You Throw Like a Girl

like many, allow countless hours of video games, movies, and television where boys witness graphic, senseless, and incessant violence of every conceivable form. The dissonance and hypocrisy is staggering. Intimacy and our natural bodies are deemed indecent and inappropriate. Yet purposeful and even gratuitous violence is perfectly okay and even shared with children as entertainment and fun.

Not all parents have acquiesced to this unsettling reality. However, there really is no avoiding this cultural dilemma. A few years ago, another friend told me about a conversation he had with his nine-year-old son and his friends. He overheard the young boys discussing a Hollywood actor and commenting that they didn't like him because, it was rumored, he was bisexual. When my friend intervened and asked the boys if they knew what that meant (assuming they had simply heard the term and didn't *really* know), they replied that the actor likes girls *and* boys. He was stunned. His amazement that nine-year-olds were discussing bisexuality was replaced with anger that this was reason enough to dislike someone. Adding to my friend's dismay was the fact that he had moved his family to a relatively small town to avoid a culture that required kids to grow up "too fast" and deal with complex social issues at early ages. He was in no way ready or prepared to discuss bisexuality with his son. He hadn't even generally discussed heterosexuality and sex with him.

THE AMERICAN FAMILY CHALLENGED

Writing about family and parental responses always brings me back to simpler times when my siblings and I lived twenty miles from New York City and our parents didn't have to worry about the negative influences outside our door. We spent hours playing games, only stopping because it got dark or the kid who owned the ball had to go home. When dinner was over (yes, we had dinner together), we would do homework, read, or play board games. During the summer, we would occasionally be allowed back outside to play backgammon under the streetlights.

Although my childhood was a few generations ago, it was half a world away. Children and parents today face a bombardment from the media and entertainment worlds that has helped distort social norms and led to a decline in decent behavior. Today's children are growing up in a culture that is dramatically more permissive than the one in which their parents were raised. And they are exposed to exponentially more representations of masculinity and more information about sex, with less parental intervention. While I learned about sex literally on the streets, kids today don't even need to leave the house. They are also exposed at much earlier ages and, in many cases, it's happening right under the noses of their parents.

The crucial question we must ask is, what do we want for our boys? Our cultural silence has made them more vulnerable and renders them defenseless against the onslaught of messages they receive through mass media. And there is almost no way to avoid this reality.

The "Streets" in the Pocket

VAST WASTELAND

The corrosive impact of media on social standards has long been debated, and while the nature of its content has grown more salacious and indecent, it's our relationship *with* media that defines one of the greatest challenges of this generation. Still, it's important to examine the "slippery slope" upon which content has plunged since the early days of television.

In 1961, the chairman of the Federal Communications Commission (FCC) verbally wagged his finger at the television industry, imploring it to do better with regard to the quality of the content it offered. Newton Minow, who was appointed by President John F. Kennedy, challenged the room of television executives to watch a full day of their own programming, uninterrupted and free of distraction. He famously assured them they would see a "vast wasteland":

> *You will see a procession of game shows, formula comedies about totally unbelievable families, blood and thunder, mayhem, violence, sadism, murder, western bad men, western good men, private eyes, gangsters, more violence, and cartoons. And endlessly, commercials—many screaming, cajoling, and offending.*

This critique still holds up today. In our media-saturated culture, the wasteland has not only grown exponentially vaster, it has also become our homeland. Popular media permeates every aspect of our lives. And while we now have the benefit of sharing collective moments that we witness en masse, we often see them through a narcissistic lens and the personal handheld devices that characterize today's generation. (Picture selfie sticks at a presidential inauguration.) Popular media no longer has viewers but "users," and content designed to be intuitive has become an extension of our beings and the very way we understand our lives. And while the online version of popular media is referred to as "social," "antisocial" seems a more accurate descriptor of its personalized nature and isolating effect.

The producers of media grow increasingly more anonymous and varied in the platforms they use. And there is no center— no accountable foundation or core. As the wasteland has grown, the controls on decency and morality have been relinquished to the individual user. And in many cases, that means children.

PORN IN THE POCKET

The fact is, there is very little we can keep from kids today. In 1977, I walked nearly two miles to see "soft" porn. In 2018, more graphic, violent, and dehumanizing pornography of every type can be accessed on the phones in their pockets.

And yet, despite decades of grandstanding claims and protests against the gratuitous sex and violence that is eroding the moral fabric of our society, the sex-and-violence industry has never been healthier—in a media environment that endlessly pushes the limits. But mere criticism of mass media will not create comprehensive measures to ease the challenges parents have historically faced to protect their children.

That is not to say that the enduring critique of mass media that began with Newton Minow's 1961 statement doesn't remain valid and necessary. We should never give up being guardians and stewards of the public spaces that media and entertainment occupy—taking a critical stance and holding content producers to account. But in our critique we also need to be honest with ourselves. We mustn't be afraid to acknowledge how our examination reveals a truth about the primal nature of our humanity, no matter how far outside our comfort zone it takes us. Doing so often uncovers the hypocrisy and rigidity of our own ideologies. We must ask: Why aren't depictions of sex, if they are supposed to reflect the true nature of our humanity, more tender and warm? What do they reveal about the impact of misogyny on portrayals of sex? We must pay attention to what this is saying about us and who we are, whether we are ready to hear it or not.

CONSIDERING PORN

Just before Newton Minow proclaimed television a "vast wasteland," he stated, "When television is good, nothing—not the theater, not the magazines or newspapers—nothing is better. But when television is bad, nothing is worse."

In the previous chapter, I suggested that masturbation was part of a healthy understanding of our bodies and ourselves as sexual beings. Some argue that pornography is contained within a "sex-positive" ideology that embraces and celebrates sexuality more freely in all its forms. I do believe in that freedom of sexual expression, and I understand how observing sexual activity excites a very real and natural human urge. However, I also subscribe to Minow's perspective: *when it's good, nothing is better; but when it's bad, nothing is worse.*

The problem is not the porn industry per se but the dogma of misogyny and masculinity that fuels its existence. Moreover, our inability to talk honestly and openly keeps all ideas about sex in the shadows as something deviant for which we should feel shame or apprehension. This gives power to porn and credibility to the ominous warning that sex is dirty, salacious, and covert. The curiosity that drove me to see *Emanuelle* was not to witness the beauty of an egalitarian portrayal of human intimacy. Or, to be more crude, it wasn't even to watch people "fuck." It was to fulfill two critical and inescapable demands of the mandate and performance of masculinity: One, it demonstrated a strong predilection for risk-taking behavior. When I was twelve years old, there was no greater opportunity to do something that was as indubitably against the rules as viewing pornography. Sneaking peeks at our father's *Playboy* magazine was one thing; actually going to the theater was the epitome of triumph over risk.

Two, it showed an adherence to the rules of misogyny.

SHE DOES NOT MATTER

Dave and I knew that seeing porn was not something you bragged about or even disclosed to girls, because although we may not have been able to articulate it, we knew it revolved around their domination and degradation. It featured what boys *do* to girls and how girls, whether they approve or not, "serve" boys. The irony of boys' early exposure to pornography is that the experience has little to do with girls. It's a misogynistic performance, a way to use women's bodies to impress other boys rather than to truly understand physical intimacy and love.

The women portrayed in porn are not real—they are not the girls in school and certainly not anyone in our families. The seemingly complicit behavior of women in porn presents a disturbing cognitive dissonance for boys: while in real life they are told to respect women, in this fictional world they witness the most disrespectful, vile, and degrading behavior. This is why boys and men will recoil when asked to imagine their mother in the porn they watch. They are aroused by what they actually view with contempt. The dissonance is shrouded in our general silence about sex.

Increasingly we are seeing cases where women's actual participation in sexual behavior is not even necessary—hence the use of date-rape drugs, including alcohol, that incapacitate and, in effect, remove women from the experience. In other words, the woman becomes inconsequential; she does not matter.

If we examine the case of Brock Turner, we hear this disturbing narrative in the defense of his crimes, from both him and his father. In 2015, nineteen-year-old Turner, an accomplished swimmer at Stanford University, raped an unconscious woman behind a dumpster. The bystanders who interrupted the attack in progress detained Turner until police arrived. They also checked to confirm that the woman was still breathing. The public outrage about the incident was not over the heinousness of the crime but the lenient sentence Turner received: just six months in jail. The judge explained that it would be "too hard" on Turner to serve a longer sentence.

As disturbing as the sentence was, so were the subsequent statements from Turner and his father. Brock Turner blamed his alcohol consumption and college party culture as factors in his raping of an unconscious woman—not his attitudes and behavior. His father suggested the sentence was too harsh for "twenty minutes of action," as if this were an actual sexual encounter. In both claims, we find a deep-seated sense of male privilege and an entitlement to women's bodies; a narrative that gets told repeatedly in pornography and the ways men understand sex.

THE PROPHECY OF GAIL DINES

Today, what was once necessarily covert behavior to access porn has become as routine and effortless as making a phone call—from anywhere, at any time.

In many ways, the ease of access to sexual content has as distorting an impact on real intimacy as porn itself. What's missing are those humanizing qualities of sexual intimacy, such as feeling awkward or embarrassed. These are important emotions in intimacy, nature's speed bumps to slow the process and allow the brain to participate as well. But as with online activity in general, online porn mutes and even dulls the emotions. The relatively anonymous way in which it is obtained and viewed presents little risk and is free of any moral interference. And finally, rarely is the user gradually introduced to online porn. A simple keyword search can launch an onslaught of extreme, violent, and misogynist images and videos, categorized by what men do to women. Taking into account all these factors, including the availability of the content to children of any age, many health officials are now examining pornography as a public health concern.

Leading this group of officials is Dr. Gail Dines, an ardent and uncompromising critic of pornography. In 2018, Dines left her position as a professor of sociology and women's studies at Wheelock College in Boston to take on the porn industry full time. She is the most eloquent and trenchant scholar on the subject and the personal and social impact it has on our lives, influencing how we see and relate to each other in our most vulnerable intimate relationships. She argues that what she calls the "pornification" of our culture, along with the silence of adults about it, has led to porn becoming a de facto source for children's sex education, as well as a force that normalizes misogyny and sexual violence.

Although many agree with Dines's assessment of porn, her warnings have been largely ignored and she is a regular target of the "pro-porn" community, criticized as a sex-hating feminist. Regardless of those opinions, it is hard not to see how her foreboding prophecies have been realized. In fact, researchers, health professionals, and practitioners increasingly talk about "porn addiction" as a real condition, even though it has not been officially designated as a disorder like other addictions (such as drug, alcohol, or gambling addiction). Like so many new social phenomena, anecdotal analysis and academic theory about porn addiction have preceded empirical evidence. Ultimately, the decision to conduct deep research of the issue is fully dependent on the honest admission of a problem. In other words, until we acknowledge that we are sexual beings and our kids are learning what sex is from pornography, our culture is truly threatened by a pornified understanding of how we fundamentally express and share intimate, physical love.

For the past three decades, I've asked college students whether they've ever had a "graphic, honest, and sustained" conversation with trusted adults about intimacy, sexual behavior, and their bodies. I started asking that question nearly ten years before the first mobile app was created. What has been most disturbing during that span of time is the continued silence of adults while a media culture has persisted in blatantly encroaching on their authority.

When I watched porn at age twelve, what I saw filled the space "between the lines" of adult conversations and provided a visual for the claims made by older, (and presumably) more knowledgeable peers. But again, the experience of today's young boys is not like mine: I walked nearly two miles to watch a porn film, and didn't see porn again until I was in college. For young boys today, the *average* age of first exposure to porn is eleven years old. This means many boys are experiencing porn well before adolescence. The porn they see is not filling gaps of information; it has become *the* informational channel, providing their foundational understanding of sexual behavior.

THE HEAT OF THE MOMENT— INFORMED BY PORN

Our most hardened attitudes and fundamental understandings of any issue rise to the surface during intense moments when there's no time for contemplative thought. This is what I referred to earlier as the "heat of the moment." For some, it is when rash decisions and mistakes are made, fights occur, and crimes are committed. However, through preparation, we can mitigate the negative impact of the heat of the moment. Repetition is the core of preparation—building intellectual and muscle memory so that in that moment, our reaction is the right one. Earlier I discussed this as the "process of sports": that meticulous process we go through to foster good decisions in the heat of the moment. This is why I began asking students if they'd had that graphic, honest, and sustained conversation with their parents. It's imperative that we examine what is informing the heat of the moment of intimacy for boys. The silence of adults, coupled with the recent proliferation of pornography, should cause urgent alarm.

And although this book can't offer a comprehensive analysis of the social and psychological impact of pornography, it is safe to say that the violent and degrading nature of much of the pornography landscape indicates a deeper problem—that of how boys are nurtured. Boys are not just receiving messages about the exploitation of women's bodies, but also the grotesque example of what they are supposed to "do." In our silence and inability to talk about sexual behavior in general, we are completely ignoring the impact of pornography on the psychosocial development of boys. The tantalizing nature of pornography—

196 ♥ You Throw Like a Girl

seeing what you've heard in rumor or what you've been told "you're not ready for"—does not tell the entire story of why porn is appealing to boys. This is especially true for young boys who have little or no experience of sexual intimacy with girls. If, for many boys, porn is their first exposure to sexual intimacy, why does sexually violent and degrading behavior make sense to them? If we have taught our boys to love and respect girls and women, why do they not reject the violence and degradation on sight?

Underlying the appeal of porn is not just learned misogyny but the low expectations boys have for their own sexual fulfillment. I am not referring to immediate carnal gratification, but fulfillment based on a profound emotional connection that is unconditional, unselfish, and truly loving. When we examine violent and degrading pornography or hear of a college athlete raping an unconscious woman, we are seeing the manifestation of the social and emotional obstruction of healthy and whole masculinity, and the emotional disconnect that perpetrators have with themselves. This traces back to my discussion of relationship abuse in Chapter Five and the question "Why does *he* stay?" If a man does not live with and use a full toolbox of emotions, then his tools for functioning in relationships are extremely limited. Likewise, if men learn about sex but are not nurtured to expect intimacy with emotional accountability to themselves and their partner, then sex for them is transactional rather than relational. This is also, in part, how a Brock Turner—a highly functioning student and athlete with Olympic aspirations—can reduce himself to raping an unconscious woman behind a dumpster.

MEDIA MATTERS

In the 1990 documentary *Dreamworlds: Gender/Sex/Power in Rock Video,* University of Massachusetts professor and film producer Dr. Sut Jhally cogently dissects the content of music videos, extrapolating the messages of violent sexism and misogyny, drawing direct links to men's violence against women. The arguments made by Jhally are undeniably compelling. The documentary was a damning and concise critique of the overwhelmingly violent misogyny and sexist content in music videos. The problem, as Jhally explained, is the monotonous and limited interpretation of violent, sex-obsessed masculinity and the hypersexualized and objectified female body. Yet Jhally does not call for more censorship; he calls for less. It is misguided to say that pornography or the mass media in general bear sole blame for fostering a rape culture and producing the likes of Brock Turner. We can't continue to scapegoat the mass media as if it's a foreign element invading our culture to corrupt the social order. It merely holds up a mirror to our cultural understanding of masculinity and sex.

When I heard Jhally's call for less censorship, I was struck by how profoundly true it was that broader interpretations of gender, sex, and a whole host of behaviors were clearly absent. Most of the images and story lines of music videos depicted gendered caricatures engaging in unhealthy and immature intimate relationships. All the anxieties of young adult relationships reduced to shallow scripts of selfish and manipulative behavior—a primary and unfortunate source of information on social behavior for an entire generation. The programming was created exclusively for young people and, in an effort to remain authentic, it was largely informed by young people who saw their idealized selves and their lives on the screen. While this approach validates the life experiences of viewers, it skews the legitimacy of youthful perspectives and dilemmas, and lacks the wisdom gained through experience and maturity that comes with living with the consequences of behavior.

Jhally's analysis was of the media that defined that genera-tion—music videos. However, more recently, mobile technology and social media have changed our concerns from content to the relationship young people have *with* media. Today, media influ-ence encourages young people to share experiences, not build and nurture relationships. This is ironic since media can make those experiences live in perpetuity. Experiences in "real life" are fleeting and temporary, and are building blocks of growth. However, fleeting moments stagnate and fester and live on the device in their pocket. Part of the devastating impact of cyber-bullying is the exaggerations of "moments" and the anonymous ways in which a moment is spread throughout a community. For the target, the moment captured in media becomes an in-escapable reality.

Like Gail Dines's caution, much of what Jhally diagnosed—how a lack of diverse interpretations of masculinity danger-ously distorts cultural expectations and understandings of male behavior—has isolated boys and narrowed and stymied their understanding of masculinity and sex even further.

ADULTS MUST WATCH

My recommendation to adults is to take the same advice New-ton Minow gave to television executives in 1961: spend a full day absorbing the media our boys consume daily. We need to withhold judgment about the programming and get past our aversion to the silly, sophomoric story lines, and consider how it may be interpreted by our boys in light of what we have or hav-en't discussed honestly and in depth with them. And we should consider all the other influences in a boy's life.

What this will likely reveal is that boys are continuously im-mersed in content that is violent, disrespectful, and hateful—all for the sake of entertainment. Boys are not simply desensitized;

this milieu has become normalized. For some boys, this content may have lost its novelty and shock value and they have grown numb to it. In fact, they may have already given it meaning and importance, social currency that has become their norm.

A strong case could be made that this content should be prohibited, but this doesn't make sense to me personally. In fact, I agree with the experts who argue that we need less censorship, not more of it. I see a connection here to how my life has not been fully represented by the sports media. I was a caricature—not a real person but a "football player." As narrow as that depiction was, it pales in comparison to the representation of masculinity by men in entertainment, which provides a more acute version of masculinity. They are the more grotesque archetypes, acting out violent, sexist behavior with limited emotion; they are masculinity incarnate. And unlike athletes, whose performance takes place in the context of a game, boys and men in entertainment portray real-life scenarios. Even in the more innocent forms of entertainment, the foundations of narrow masculinity are present: common themes and comments are homophobic or involve dynamics where "boys rule" or have more social freedom than girls. It may not be as demonstrably sexist today as when I was a boy (the nearly all-boy cast of my favorite show back then, *The Little Rascals*, had something called the "He-Man Women Haters Club"), but it is still difficult to find content that adequately represents whole, healthy masculinity.

The way in which ratings are applied to content is important to understand. In 1968, the Motion Picture Association of America established a rating system to notify audiences about "mature content" in film. In 1994, the Entertainment Software Rating Board was formed in response to violence in video games. The FCC's guidelines for television went into effect in 1997 and have since become the standard rating system for cable and online television programs. In each case, ratings most often warn of graphic and gratuitous violence and explicit sexual content. We deem certain images, language, and stories to be appropriate by age—as if raping and killing and all the preceding behaviors are appropriate for *any* age. Yes, it may be true that certain content is too sophisticated for younger people with fewer life experiences, and older people have the right to view what they want. Yet ratings don't intend to protect intellectual development but instead govern (the assumed) sensibilities of social decency.

THE OBJECTIFICATION OF MEN

This, in many ways, is where the myth of masculinity is advanced. Over the years, this approach to controlling "mature content" has resulted in a deepening of the myth and performance of masculinity. We are entertained and distracted by caricatures of masculinity while we ignore our true humanity. We laugh at the shortcomings of men who don't meet the mandate and are entertained by those who fail in the attempt to be whole, loving men. And we are relentlessly reminded of what mythological hypermasculinity looks like; the hyperbole of risk-taking, violence, and unemotional sexualized masculinity is celebrated. The objectification of muscular male bodies has not been framed as a commercial tool quite as harshly as women's bodies but it is no less present in the lives of boys—telling them what a (real) man's body is "supposed" to look like. Augmenting the conflated images of physicality and masculinity is the ever-present addition of weaponry that continues to grow more lethal and destructive. Filmmaker Jeremy Earp calls it "prosthetic masculinity," as it often replaces a weaponized muscular body with that of a weapon that becomes an extension of the violent persona.

The incessant images of violent men and exaggerated and predatory sexual prowess have distorted and desensitized the reality, discourse, and ultimate understanding of both sex and violence: sex is seen as dirty (but desirable) and violence is glorified and purposeful. In reality, violence is the forceful attempt to control nature and an evil way to extinguish life. We have become more at ease with, and even entertained by, witnessing unnatural death while admonishing the beauty of how life is formed and loving existence is shared.

I believe we need a different approach to how we rate content to help parents be more intentional than defensive. The current system, self-managed by those who produce the content, often puts parents in a defensive position. With the ease of access children have to different media, parents are rendered virtually defenseless in managing what children are exposed to. A rating system should provide more information and not be driven by concerns of "age-appropriateness"; rather, it should focus on giving parents a "choice" of content that is healthy and aspirational. There is a reliable body of research and social science regarding prosocial behavior that could guide this approach. Such a system would thus recognize the ways that the mass media, in all its incarnations but especially social and mobile media, can help inform our ideologies, attitudes, cultural norms, and sense of self.

SEXISM IN PRINT

In the summer of 2005, I was invited to a meeting by a cable television network geared to children and early adolescents. The meeting was meant to explore the idea of healthier programming for boys. I was encouraged that the executives at the network recognized the leap from innocence to violence that most boys experience through media. They were seeking advice on how to appeal to boys without reinforcing the messages of "toxic masculinity" they realized were in so much of their programming for that population. Dr. William Pollack, author of *Real Boys: Rescuing our Sons from the Myths of Boyhood,* and I spent several hours with production and creative executives outlining the "state of masculinity" and explaining how boys are negatively impacted by narrow interpretations of masculinity. It was a productive meeting, yet I was haunted by the feeling that this was an exercise in futility, that the idealized masculinity Dr. Pollack and I described was not something the network could develop in its programming.

While networks geared toward young audiences have rightfully struggled to feature healthy images and stories for boys, the broader media environment has remained indifferent. Tampering with strongly held beliefs makes stories less appealing and jeopardizes commercial appeal. And again, the ease of access to detrimental content ensures that its proliferation continues. Meanwhile, positive counter-messages about healthy, whole masculinity fail to reach boys. But that isn't because those messages don't exist or aren't fighting to be heard.

When Jackson Katz and I appeared on *The Oprah Winfrey Show*, after I was featured in her magazine in 2002, we believed it would prove to be a defining moment in our work. But as I've mentioned, when Oprah recommended me to a publisher, I got his attention, but not his consideration. The written response was quick and very discouraging. I was not discouraged as a writer or even as an advocate; I know that writing a book is a lengthy and arduous endeavor. I was discouraged as a caring man, and on behalf of all caring men. In his letter, the rationale he gave for rejecting my work was literary cowardice. It read:

Thanks so much for letting us review your manuscript for YOU THROW LIKE A GIRL. Your cause is such a good one, and the attention it is receiving in O and on Oprah will certainly help get your message out in a big way. Our concern about the book, however, is that those who agree with your message won't feel the need to read a book in order to be convinced, while those who really need it would not buy one. It's a dilemma we don't think we could solve, but I hope you find a publishing house that feels more able to do so.

This was a familiar response to my manuscript, both before and after I was featured on the show and in the magazine. Even though the publicity raised the profile of my work with women, I continued to hear from editors, agents, and publishers that the market was not men but twenty-five- to forty-year-old, college-educated white women. One woman actually told me that *she* was the market and wanted me to convince her why she should buy my book.

The advocate in me understood this reaction to my manuscript, but once again, the caring man in me was insulted by the dismissive position that men don't care or would not seek out such information. I am fully aware that men don't want to talk publicly about this issue—that is the essence of the performance of masculinity. But I also know men continue to seek knowledge to be better partners and fathers. What the book industry chooses to publish and not to publish reveals a troubling sexism working against men about what they read, and even perpetuates the misconception that they don't read at all. Take, for instance, the popularity of *Heaven's Fury*, coauthored by Curtis James Jackson III (better known as the rapper 50 Cent), and G-Unit Books, the Simon & Schuster imprint through which it was released. How many twenty-five- to forty-year-old, college-educated white women are picking up 50 Cent's latest musing to read while curled up in front of the fire?

Even if his writing is extraordinary—which it may be, considering that G-Unit Books has published many of his titles—I am both jealous and outraged. Don't tell me that a book about the examination of masculinity—with the goal of nurturing loving, healthy, nonviolent boys and men—has no market, but the book that perpetuates the narrative of violent, poor black masculinity has a broad market among white women with college degrees. And don't tell me that my market is college-educated white women of a certain age and that I should modify my writing to appeal to their sensibilities. I am aware of the needs and perspectives of grandmothers, mothers, aunts, sisters, and daughters trying to understand their relationships with the men in their lives. But we must also focus on the needs of grandfathers, fathers, brothers, uncles, brothers, and sons, to help them work toward creating a healthy understanding of loving masculinity.

Sadly, not only are boys today continually exposed to a narrow interpretation of masculinity in the mass media, but we have also stifled a conversation of growth, maturity, and evolving masculinity among adult men. There is one thing of which I am certain about most fathers, male coaches, and educators—they care about developing healthy and whole men. They want to be transformative influences on the next generation of boys, and they want more information on how to do that. But they are often overwhelmed by a prevailing and narrow view of masculinity that is consistent with how they were raised. In many ways, they themselves struggle with understanding and reconciling their relationships with their fathers and untangling what it means to be a whole man. This confusion is perpetuated by mass media and exacerbated by their lived experiences—their "old-school" dads and coaches and traditions of silence. If more men grasped the messages they were actually feeding boys, and the ways that popular culture reinforces those messages, they would rethink parenting styles, media and entertainment, coaching, sports, and a litany of other things that our patriarchal culture fails to critically examine that are the conduit tools by which masculinity is learned and passed on to future generations.

CONCLUSION
Be Your Son's Father,
Not Your Father's Son

RUDOLPH GENE McPHERSON

My parents raised five children, all born before 1965, in suburban Long Island, New York. I am the youngest and the third son. My father's influence is evident in all of the boys. Although it manifests differently in each of us, we all possess an aloof, pragmatic stubbornness that is a bit self-righteous. Our independence and determination were unmistakable in the ways each of us charged through our childhood years, most especially when it came to sports. Miles, the second child and oldest boy, played football and became the first player ever drafted into the NFL out of the University of New Haven. Mark, the middle child, played football until the 1976 Summer Olympic boxing team sparked his passion for boxing. In 1986, he was ranked number two in the world as a junior middleweight fighter. At the same time, I was playing at Syracuse on the verge of a professional career of my own.

From the outside, it may sound like I came from an amazing sports family, but it never felt that way to me. While sports dominated our days, it never felt bigger than our family. Perhaps it was because I never once heard my father take credit for producing such athletically gifted men. In fact, the thought of my father bragging about his sons is inconceivable. When I asked him why he never took credit for our athletic success, he shrugged it off, as if it were a mystery.

What was not a mystery was how he taught us the love of play. We were typical athletic boys, and he played with us because he enjoyed playing. He dragged us out into the street or to the park with our uncles, not because he was trying to make us better, but because he simply loved doing so.

He loved baseball. I will never forget the summer I began playing as a pitcher. While he sat in a crouch mimicking New York Mets catcher Jerry Grote, he coached me to pitch like Grote's teammate, the great Tom Seaver. We had none of the proper equipment and lived on a straight street with a long incline. Without fail, when a ball got past him, he would turn and chase it, no matter how far down the hill my wayward curveball traveled. The inconvenience didn't faze him. Instead, he was focused and determined to make the next pitch better, delivering tips and suggestions as he returned the ball to me and resumed his catcher stance.

I distinctly remember feeling amazed and grateful for his selflessness and patience. *This can't be fun for him,* I frequently thought as he chased balls down the hill. But then, later in life, I heard him tell stories of his childhood in Jamaica and having no one to play with. He would hit balls and then go find them in a field, only to aimlessly hit the ball again. There was no discernible game, no structure, and no opponent for whom he was preparing . . . it was just him.

Growing up in Jamaica, his father was a prominent musician and successful businessman. He had the money and status to provide well for his family. In fact, as a child, my father and his brother attended the finest boarding school on the island. They spent the school year across the island from their parents, receiving a privileged education not afforded every Jamaican. My grandfather, Milton McPherson, was the leader of his own big band and part owner of the Silver Slipper nightclub in Jamaica, and was well known throughout the Caribbean. His fame brought higher social status and the opportunity for a better life. Ultimately, this meant a move to the United States. In 1944, he and my grandmother left his family and came to America. Three years later, my father and his brother joined them in Brooklyn, New York.

The irony of having this privileged boarding school experience was that it took the children away from their parents. When my father did spend time with his father, it was usually not a warm experience. It was the norm in Jamaica and in those days that children were not the center of attention. Listening to my father tell it, the purpose of sending them away to boarding school was to prepare them to return as adults, ready to participate in the culture.

My grandparents left them on the island alone for three years. My father recalled that time with a feeling of abandonment. It didn't matter that the people around him (including the nuns at their school) believed he and his brother were privileged; after all, they would also be heading to America soon. My father considered those the most difficult years of his life. Separated from his parents, they spent holidays and summers at school, the only two students without a home base to reconnect with tradition, family, and love. The conspicuous silence of empty dining halls, playgrounds, and hallways characterized the period of my dad's life from age ten to thirteen when he says he "died on the vine." As he reflected on those years as an adult, he said it was all he knew, so of course he gritted his teeth and endured. Even in his later years, he still expressed special sympathy for orphans and kids who are unloved.

My father was not unloved. His parents made great sacrifices to provide a better life for their children. Hundreds of miles away, my grandfather gave up his music and took a job on a farm. As many American men were oversees fighting World

War II, the best way for an immigrant man to stay in the country was to take jobs left by servicemen. Ultimately, he became an accountant and, as I remember, only played piano on rare occasions. When I think of the amount of time my dad lost with his father, I wonder how much of my grandfather's sacrifices were worth it.

The emotional disconnect in my father was as present in his personality as his ethnicity, especially during family holidays. However, when it came to playing, he was always ready for a catch or a discussion of the physical mechanics of sports. He was a good athlete who ran track briefly in college and had a short-lived boxing career, so even though he never took credit for our success, he enjoyed that we all played sports for most of his life. The way he expressed love and affection was often in the silent participation of playing. Mark used to say that the only reason our father wanted to have kids was to have someone to play with. In fact, one of my fondest memories was a moment when we were just four guys playing ball.

It was Christmas Day 1985, a balmy fifty degrees in New York. Miles was home from San Diego (the Chargers didn't make the playoffs), and I returned from Syracuse after a disappointing bowl loss with my team. Naturally, in the midst of such great weather, my father roused us for a game at the local park. It was not enough for him just to play catch; he demanded we make a game out of it. So, Mark and Miles set up on defense, I played quarterback, and my father was my wide receiver. During the game, he asked me to give him routes and pass patterns, as if he understood the offense I ran at Syracuse. He was in decent shape then, and at one point he asked for a deep route, figuring he could surprise Miles and run past him. For about twenty yards, he looked real smooth . . . until he pulled his hamstring.

We all limped home that day—a boxer in perpetual pain,

two football players bruised from a four-month season, and their father experiencing the pain of watching his sons usurp his reign of physical dominance. But at least he had someone to play with.

When I was in the fourth grade, long after he put a second floor on our house to accommodate the growing family, he broke ground on a new pool. I can vividly remember the planning process: blueprint diagrams, fencing specifications, and, of course, the diving board and lining pattern. But in all the years of meticulous upkeep, of decorative rocks, finely trimmed shrubbery, and pH level balance, one thing struck me as odd. I never saw my father relax by the pool. He worked on it tirelessly, but never enjoyed it. In fact, about once a year he would actually go for a swim. Invariably, his wallet would be on the clothesline afterward, because he had never actually planned to take a dip. Rather, his plunge would come after hours of sweating in the hot sun, working beside fifty thousand gallons of pristine, cool water. *Ah, screw it*, was the declaration in his head before he dove in, clothes, wallet, and all. For him, the pool was not his source of enjoyment. His enjoyment came from providing the pool for *us*. For him, it only served as a temporary relief from that responsibility, the epitome of dutiful masculinity.

Early in life, my father was an enigma. He did so much for us, yet aside from playing ball, he seemed not to enjoy himself. He also shared so little of himself. He worked hard, not asking much of us while doing what he needed to give us a better life than the one he had. As with his own parents, I'm sure this is the noble intention of every generation. But it offers very little to go on in terms of what is actually expected from the next generation. The lack of dialogue left so much to interpretation.

CONVERSATIONS WITH POP

As I got older, I realized that one of the benefits of being the youngest of five siblings was that in interactions with either of my parents, especially my dad, I got less "parent" and more of a raw, authentic adult. We discussed serious topics on a daily basis. As early as middle school, we had conversations about each major decision regarding my future, like when I chose to transfer school districts simply for the sake of playing for a better football team. It was a lengthy process with a great deal to consider, and in the end, it was my decision. The process was repeated when I chose a college, hired an agent, and bought my first car. It's hard to put into words what his trust in my judgment and respect for my decisions did for my self-confidence.

My father's influence is evident in my speaking style. I have always managed to address complex and difficult issues with an idiosyncratic levity that characterized most of our interactions. Our conversations were always intellectually compelling yet sprinkled with dry humor. Very rarely did he impose his worldview on me. He always presented his arguments with a pragmatic and objective consideration of the facts. When he took a position, it was definitive but almost self-satisfied in that he didn't care if you agreed. I remember sensing that he was always curious about how I was experiencing and interpreting the world because he knew it was different from the one in which he'd been raised—although there was that one time when my perspective pushed his patience.

During one of our existential conversations about racism, the state of America, and the pressing social issues of the time, I expressed an opinion that made him somewhat uncomfortable. I felt his discomfort through the phone, but pressed on. He grew more and more silent until finally he interrupted: "Yes, Donald, but you have the—" He dropped off as abruptly as he'd begun.

I knew what he wanted to say so I finished, "I have the luxury to think that way, right?"

"Yes," he replied.

To which I added, "Yes, that's right, I do—and that is a luxury I have because of *you*!"

He worked hard so that we would have a better childhood, a better life, than he'd had as a child. There is no denying how well he achieved that for my siblings and me, but I'm just not sure if he truly understood his role in shaping my ability to fully appreciate and maximize the opportunity his life afforded mine.

It was not until I reached adulthood that I came to understand the depth of his sensitivity and how firmly rooted and concealed it was in his identity. When I interviewed him for this book, he told me there were times, unbeknownst to our family, when he would leave the room because a television show or commercial made him emotional and he was afraid he would cry in front of his children. He didn't just hide his emotions, he literally hid *with* them. A few years after my father died, I learned from my mother that he actually left the stands during a football game because he was overcome with emotion. After a very hard hit, I lay unconscious for a few minutes. When I regained consciousness, my first thought was of my family in the stands, so I made a gesture that I knew my brother and father would interpret as an indication that I was okay. I figured they would laugh and react with their characteristically blunt humor that bordered on being cruel. Never did I consider that my dad was pacing the stadium concourse in tears.

My father hid his emotions well, but he did not hide his caring. It may have been awkwardly expressed at times, but there was a real effort on his part to be a better father than his own dad. That didn't stem from any animus toward him; rather, he wanted to offer us the love and attention he did not receive from his parents. Although his parents failed to overtly express that love, he felt it nonetheless and understood it as a form of love defined by the culture and times in which he was raised.

Despite doing so much to give us the things he did not have as a boy, he still struggled to give us certain things we really needed from him. He gave us plenty of time—time he never had with his dad—but that time often lacked emotion. That is easy to see now, but it was the norm then, just as it was normal not to attend the birth of any of his children or ever change a diaper. The role of fathers was quite different in the 1970s. The expectations of their participation as nurturers and caregivers were minimal; therefore, my father had little reason to reconsider his role.

But so much has changed since then. Arguably, one of the greatest challenges facing parents, and fathers in particular, are the rapidly changing social norms around gender. This is not simply about changing diapers or the new occupational roles that men must assume in a technological age. Nor is it simply about the advancement of women in areas once considered men's domain, or the imperative to confront systemic gender violence and inequality.

By choice, men have been left behind in an important conversation about gender roles, behavioral expectations, and the way that behavior is policed in our society. This is a collective blind spot, and as an unintended outcome of privilege, men have been allowed to "opt out" of a public discussion regarding the expectations placed on their own expanding roles and responsibilities. This problem is further exacerbated if men do not understand that they are gendered beings influenced by and living on a gender spectrum.

MARRIAGE "EQUALITY"

In 2003, Massachusetts became the first state to legalize same-sex marriage. By 2015, it was legal in all fifty states. While many opponents maintain that same-sex marriage threatens the institution of (heterosexual) marriage, I have always seen a deeper motivation in the fight to deny people who love each other their fundamental rights as partners: what opponents actually want is to uphold marriage as a tool of patriarchy.

There are examples people often point to illustrating the patriarchal traditions of traditional marriage, such as the protective wedding ritual of a father "giving away" his daughter to the groom, symbolically transferring power over her life, and the convention of a wife losing her family name to assume her husband's, thereby affixing her identity and worth to his. In fact, there are a host of other social, religious, economic, and legal ways that marriage is governed by patriarchy. Essentially, removing the dogma of heterosexuality's exclusive claim on marriage takes power and control away from men. But contrary to what opponents believe, same-sex marriage actually strengthens the idea of marriage, as it necessarily emphasizes the requirement of a mutual partnership—true marriage "equality."

It is in this mutual partnership where the need for men to live in their wholeness is critical. But this is difficult for the current generation of men who have had few role models or examples of what that evolving role looks like. We have programs and discussions about dads and daughters driven by the movement to raise safe and healthy girls, but this is consistent with the mode of protective patriarchy that fails to recognize a greater risk factor to girls' health—unhealthy boys. What about a father's influence on a son's healthy development to become a whole person and, eventually, a partner in a true egalitarian relationship?

Our current generation of fathers is challenged with learning to perform tasks and assume roles we never witnessed our fathers doing. It's interesting to hear older men refer to a father's time alone with his own child as "babysitting." The implication is beyond subtle: the role they are referring to, one typically performed by the thirteen-year-old girl next door, is temporary and comes with limited authority and low performance expectations.

Some people believe that the changing gender dynamics are emasculating for men, which clearly exemplifies the patriarchal notion that gender equality represents an abdication of men's power. Instead of us blaming women for our "emasculation," we should consider how the demands of the mandate of masculinity render us incapable of viewing women as our equals. To borrow a phrase, many men have grandmothers, mothers, daughters, wives, and partners, and they are not adversaries bent on our destruction. Women are not the "enemy"; it's not an either/or proposition. Men must also recognize that in the fight for gender equality, women have an ever-growing ally—men. The dogmatic and rigid way in which men consider gender is changing, even in our most draconian male environments. This has accelerated social change more quickly than many are prepared for, and while progress can be debated, it cannot be ignored.

COURAGE TO BE VULNERABLE

In 1934, a Jewish boy named Richard Raskind was born in New York City. His mother was a professor at Columbia University and one of the first female psychiatrists in the United States. His father was an orthopedic surgeon. Raskind was a three-sport athlete (football, baseball, swimming) at Horace Mann High School and went on to Yale, where he captained the tennis team. After college, Raskind pursued his medical career with a specialization in ophthalmology, studying and working in the most renowned hospitals and medical centers in the country. Raskind later joined the US Navy and, in addition to continuing his medical training, won the all-Navy tennis championship. But none of this is what brought Raskind notoriety.

Richard Raskind entered the consciousness of the American public as Renée Richards, a forty-one-year-old transgender woman petitioning the World Tennis Association to compete as a woman. I remember in 1977 when Richards was first allowed to compete in the US Open. At the time we called it a "sex-change operation" and I cannot recall a single mature or respectful utterance by any adult about what that entailed or meant to her life. I'm not sure anyone I knew considered what was actually happening in her life beyond the game of tennis. Even though I know everyone had opinions, they were never discussed openly. I think about Richards often these days as I reflect on how much more informed and understanding our culture has become about LGBTQ awareness and rights. I also wonder what Richards was thinking as Caitlyn Jenner transitioned before our eyes: an Olympic hero once on the Wheaties box, then a bizarre reality-TV star, then a pop culture icon. In the span of what felt like a few months, Bruce Jenner underwent reassignment surgery, declared her identity as Caitlyn, and, in a turn of events Renée Richards could never have imagined for herself, was honored by ESPN with an ESPY Award for her courage.

"Courage" is the quintessential marker of the mandate of masculinity. Vulnerability may be the most difficult for men to understand or demonstrate, but courage requires overt, purposeful, and selfless action. We often mistakenly view "manhood" as a fixed destination, a finite set of jobs and roles, but it's more like a journey, one not defined simply by enduring or persevering but by fully embracing the journey itself. And true courage is demonstrably and unashamedly living our wholeness throughout the journey.

Courage, like the handful of other characteristics used to narrowly define masculinity, is largely viewed through a small lens, typically as it relates to facing physical violence or harm. ESPN's recognition of Jenner's courage to live in her truth and in her wholeness despite the immense social pressures she faced as an iconic male athlete was culturally significant because it recognized a broader definition of courage. Jenner's reality reflected a collective and unspoken truth: gender is such a manifestly fluid reality in our families and communities that it can and should no longer be confined or ignored.

Renée Richards was a true pioneer of great courage. Caitlyn Jenner represents the power of the media to expose the traditions of silence in our culture. Neither of them was a social aberration. Access to the media simply enabled Jenner a platform from which she could not be ignored and through which our culture could recognize the trans community like it never had before.

No matter where we fall on the spectrum of promoting or fighting for social change, the fact remains that it's happening and we must collectively grapple with the discomfort caused by a shift from the way "things have always been." However, in this age of social media, our online discourse is not always helping social progress; we are too often divided into different echo chambers where our perspectives are hardened and polarized. While change typically comes at the "tip of a spear," progress has been found in the patience and mutual respect to listen to each other and advance toward a reasonable understanding and expression of truth. This applies to every generation that has strived to be better than the one in which it was raised. On every issue, from the environment to education to health care, we are better and have grown by having access to more information and smarter ways of looking at how "things have always been." And on so many social issues—including race and gender—we must be honest and respectful of the lives and perspectives of those around us that inform the ways we improve and grow.

This is one more place where privilege creates a sad and

unfortunate "blind spot" for men: the disabling of our ability to guide the next generation of boys toward their wholeness. Privilege removes the appetite and incentive for seeking new information because it may dismantle the way "things have always been," thus threatening the power and privilege of patriarchy. Once again, the underlying privilege of masculinity is that it's derived by the degradation of women. Masculinity is defined not in its wholeness but too often by what it is not. Hence the understanding that *we don't raise boys to be men, we raise them not to be women . . . or gay men.*

What does whole and healthy masculinity look like? And what are the incentives to encourage men to embrace a different way of looking at masculinity as we raise the next generation of boys? Naturally, there is great risk in the proposition of challenging how we raise boys, especially if it disrupts a status quo or dismantles important and venerated beliefs and traditions. How do we mitigate the impact of that risk in a ways that leads to honest and productive dialogue? During a presentation to a college football team, I offered my analysis of the insult "You throw like a girl," and a young man responded with a challenge: "Yes, but if your son threw like a girl, wouldn't you do something about it?" I could hear in his tone his profound resolution. In his view, the act of throwing was not only a "gender-normal" behavior and an inherently male trait, but it also carried social capital. He supposed that if this son he imagined I had lacked the gendered skill of throwing, I would be faced with a salient dilemma: my failure to teach my son to "throw normal" meant I was derelict in fulfilling my essential role as a father.

I quickly responded, "I am not going to make my son better by degrading my daughter." I had given that session to address the issue of men's violence against women; therefore, I had to confront the idea that such language fundamentally degrades women and is foundational to men's violence against women. It was a sharp retort, but my answer was incomplete. It did not give them anything upon which they could build.

I left that session with a weighty and consuming question that has driven the mission of my work ever since: how do we raise healthy and whole boys without degrading girls in the process? It is a challenge for all men, but one particularly vital in my work and life.

INTENTIONAL MASCULINITY AND DELIBERATIVE TEACHING

I am often asked how and when I came to this work and about my particular perspective of confronting the mandate of masculinity. People assume that I had an epiphany born out of some profound experience that led to gender enlightenment. But there was no "moment," as I've mentioned. I was twenty-nine years old when I began to learn and grow, although I was still a participant in the performance of masculinity and in many ways struggling to reconcile with the foundation of my identity and the ways "things have always been." But I began to come to terms with how deeply ingrained the mandate of masculinity was and how misogyny and sexism had influenced so many aspects of my life.

In the course of my work, I've met boys and young men whose healthy masculine identity developed much earlier in life, as high school or college students. These were not just kind men by nature; instead, they recognized and confronted the myriad social pressures to adhere to sexist values. As a result, they are now empathetic, vulnerable, and kind, and also tough, strong, and sometimes athletic. Notably, all of these men share one thing in common: they were nurtured in a way that valued their wholeness as people above their performance as men.

On rare occasions when I get to meet the adults who have influenced these boys and men, I feel a strong compulsion to delve into their parenting strategies. Whether they were single mothers or fathers, same-sex couples, or heterosexual couples, these parents all raised their boys deliberately, with a keen sense that the mandate of masculinity was a destructive force. Some had experienced neglect or abuse at the hands of their father or another man and wanted the opposite experience for their children. Some had a loving father or male figure in their lives who had demonstrated empathy and compassion along with patriarchal "tough love," and as parents chose to only hold on to the former. Although their motivations may have differed, again, the common thread was the deliberate way they raised their boys. They did not leave their sons to learn the rules of masculinity from a culture steeped in privileged patriarchy. They also held accountable the influences on their sons outside the home, such as their teachers and coaches.

Their boys were not competing to be the alpha male in grade school and on the playground. If they viewed other boys with jealousy, disdain, or fear, they did not act on it and therefore their identity wasn't dependent on or validated by those emotions. Most importantly, they were not shamed by their fathers or adult men in their lives. Their rejection of the mandate was wholly and lovingly supported, and it didn't damage their self-esteem or resilience; they were no less of a boy. This is not to say they did not acknowledge or understand the pressure to conform or even feel it themselves. But it was not enough to compromise the wholeness they had been deliberately raised and encouraged to embrace.

We are capable of achieving this for all boys. The "secret ingredient" isn't really a secret. It is a matter of intentionally holding to the set of values and behaviors we all hope to instill in our children to guide them through a healthy and happy life. But we cannot simply assume boys are "okay" or that this is just how they are supposed to be. Nor can we continue to ignore what we know because it makes us uncomfortable.

We are wiser than previous generations and make better decisions regarding our diet and health, cutting back on toxic habits like eating processed foods and smoking. Our lives have improved largely because we have more and more accurate information. We prepare and execute at a higher level in the workplace by using more precise data, which we now access at greater volumes and speeds. We use information previously unavailable about weather, travel, and global events. We must apply this same process of gathering essential information to how we raise and nurture future generations of boys.

This process sheds light on that exchange I had with the college football player years ago. When he asked me what I would do if my son threw like a girl, my first thought was about the mechanics of throwing a football, and how pivotal the learning process is in acquiring this skill. The oblong shape of a football and the way in which the game is played make throwing a football so different from other kinds of balls. The mechanics begin with the feet and involve the entire body, right up to the release at the tip of the index finger. Last to touch the ball, the index finger is crucial to producing the spiral, taking the wobble out of the ball in flight.

I have taught both girls and boys how to throw a football, and boys are almost always initially much more difficult to teach than girls. Most boys believe that throwing a ball is their birthright (that gendered trait), and if they falter, all they have to do is try harder. In their heads, they know what the quarterback looks like in action and they have mastered the motor movements. However, they lack the precise mechanics to produce a spiral. Most of the girls I have taught, on the other hand, have listened carefully and applied the techniques they learned in proper sequence. Unlike the boys, they weren't trying to mimic a football player they admire, which can cloud the learning process. In every one of those cases, to "throw like a girl" meant throwing the proper way.

Years after that exchange with the football player, during a meeting at the Pentagon, I shared the story with the judge advocate general of the Air Force. I mentioned what I had gleaned watching girls learn to throw a football. He smiled in agreement: he had witnessed the inclusion of women in Air Force training programs. "If we can train women to fly our planes and drop bombs with precision," he said, "we can teach men to be better gentlemen."

LESSONS FROM JOHN GLENN

During the past three decades, I have grown increasingly critical of the role of sports in American culture, especially as it pertains to children. My critique is not because I had a regretful experience. In fact, I still truly love sports, and that is why I am often critical. One of my key targets is the way youth sports have undervalued the importance of practice and preparation, and how parents have been deceived and manipulated by their hopes for their children's success. As an educator who uses the platform and appeal of sports to teach, I find this distortion of priorities troubling. And as my understanding of masculinity has evolved, and I've seen how sports perpetuate the worst myths about it, my critique has only grown sharper.

During a moment when I was looking for wisdom on this issue, I found it upon meeting one of my heroes in life, US senator and Mercury Seven astronaut John Glenn, which occurred on that evening in 2008 when we were both honored by the National Football Foundation. I was a junior in college when I first considered Glenn's historic feat. I saw the film *The Right Stuff*, chronicling the selection of America's first team of astronauts, the Mercury Seven, and I was fascinated. I identified with Glenn's personality and demeanor. It became one of those films I would watch occasionally as fodder for my football dreams. It would motivate me to live for something greater than myself. Through the hyperbole of sports, I could compare a Saturday-afternoon game to being among the first group of human beings to travel into outer space. I imagined I too had "the right stuff"—those fundamental qualities that enabled ordinary men to reach extraordinary heights.

On February 20, 1962, John Glenn was the lone pilot aboard the *Friendship 7* and became the first American to orbit our planet. On December 9, 2008, he and I shared the stage at the Waldorf Astoria in New York City at the College Football Hall of Fame awards dinner. He received the Gold Medal Award and I was inducted into the Hall of Fame. Despite the amazing honor and grandeur of having my football career celebrated, meeting Senator Glenn was the highlight of my night. It was also the moment he destroyed the movie I loved, though he did so for all the right reasons.

I did my best to keep my cool as I approached Senator Glenn, but I also wanted to give him the proper reverence he commanded. He was gracious and the celebratory atmosphere of the evening made the conversation easy. I was delightfully relieved that my hero was indeed "forthright, gracious, and magnanimous" (a line from the film). I wanted to walk away before that impression was ruined, but as images of *The Right Stuff* and all my favorite scenes with astronaut John Glenn filled my head, I could not contain myself. I blurted something like, "*The Right Stuff* is my favorite movie!" (Actually, it's *Jaws*, but he didn't need to know that.) He paused, squared his body, and sharply expressed his disapproval of the film, adding that *Apollo 13* was better.

For those not familiar, *Apollo 13* tells the story of what was essentially a failed space mission. Damage to the capsule during liftoff forced the crew to abandon their mission to land on and explore the moon. The crew was then faced with an entirely new mission—getting back to earth in a highly compromised spacecraft. Proceeding through a series of checklists, the crew had to determine which parts and systems were still functional, and how they could be repurposed to make them operational for their new mission.

Seeming to be back in the moment, Senator Glenn lit up as he talked about the process of preparing for a mission and the courage required to sit on what is effectively a bomb that would propel him into outer space on a tiny aircraft, realizing that, to quote fellow Mercury Seven astronaut Alan Shepard, "one's safety factor was determined by the lowest bidder on a government contract." This is the kind of courage I referred to earlier—bravery in the face of the threat of death or grave harm. Separate from that, Glenn asserted that the real work lay in the process of preparation for all those things that might go wrong. He talked about visiting the factories where every part of the spacecraft was manufactured and tested so he and his fellow astronauts knew how to work backward with every piece of the ship in the event that any one piece failed. He talked about all the painstaking and meticulous drilling, testing, and more drilling. Then he referred back to *Apollo 13*. As the entire world looked on with trepidation for the fate of the men and their mission, more than two hundred thousand miles from earth, the crew went through their checks.

The process Glenn talked about is summed up by something else Alan Shepard said: "You probably spend more time in planning and training and designing for things to go wrong, and how you cope with them, than you do for things to go right." This is precisely the essence of sports and the process of preparation that anticipates the heat of the moment. Preparation is rooted in striving for excellence while honestly considering the reality of all possible outcomes.

Shepard's statement is a recognition of one's vulnerability, weakness, and lack of complete control. It's also a recognition that in every circumstance, being able to utilize every tool available, and knowing how to apply them, especially in the heat of the moment, is an absolute requisite for success—whether you are an astronaut, an athlete, or simply a human. It doesn't matter how great or small the challenge.

Although Senator Glenn destroyed the image I had from afar, he perfectly framed my feelings about sports and masculinity in a different context and in an empowering way. He encapsulated what I was trying to achieve in my mission to not just debunk myths about masculinity, but to elevate the way in which we engage each moment with our best (and best prepared) selves. For me, this means honestly recognizing the limits of how masculinity is currently defined and aspiring to live differently, embracing and utilizing more tools such as empathy, sensitivity, and vulnerability. Lastly, he reinforced my resolve to pursue the answer to how we raise healthy and whole sons without degrading our daughters.

Certainly, Senator Glenn had to be tough, strong, and a master of his emotions. Similarly, Eileen Collins—who, on February 3, 1995, became the first woman to command a space shuttle—called upon those same qualities in her own leadership role. Her success, like that of so many women who have excelled in roles and environments once considered the dominion of men, embodies the wholeness of humanity. Women athletes, elected officials, corporate leaders, and members of the armed services have proven that the wholeness of humanity is demonstrating that being tough, strong, and physically dominant does not supplant or diminish the ability to be loving, caring, and vulnerable. Men must likewise recognize that being caring and loving makes us better partners, bosses, and leaders. Sensitivity and empathy make us better listeners and healthier about our own needs and emotional and physical health, not to mention that of the people in our lives. Embracing and understanding vulnerability makes us better fathers. We are not reduced as men by deliberately demonstrating these qualities; rather, we are made whole.

TO BE A MAN—LOVING, JOYFUL

During one particular visit to a college, following a morning session with a football team, I conducted a session with professional staff on the same campus. It was a large, mixed-gender staff of social workers, counselors, and advisors from various departments on campus. During an overview that included what I had discussed in the morning session, I asked the group the same question I asked the football team: "What does it mean to 'be a man'?" The response from this group of caring, sensitive, and highly trained men in the room was no different than the football team's, touching on all the stereotypical attributes reflected in the box of masculinity. I pressed them, asking if in their daily work with young people, did they not demonstrate empathy, vulnerability, and sensitivity? As I drilled further, they explained that in their jobs they utilized those qualities, but as men, they ignored them. It was a revealing moment. They used phrases such as, "You know, it's different when I'm with the guys." They were stuck in that place of performing masculinity for other men even when it belied their true identities.

Years later, I had the opportunity to once again ask a group of men what they thought it meant "to be a man." In this instance, I was asked to participate in a panel discussion of fathers whose boys attended a private school on Long Island. Before the panel there was a screening of the film *The Mask You Live In,* a brilliant documentary on masculinity produced by Jennifer Siebel Newsom and Jessica Congdon. I immediately accepted the invitation but with a caveat that I could spend time with the dads who volunteered before the event. They agreed. On a cold, rainy November evening, a diverse group of men trudged through New York City rush-hour traffic to discuss a film they had not yet seen and that would challenge their notions of masculinity. And that discussion would be with a man they had not yet met, who was going to talk about their roles as fathers.

When I ultimately asked them for their definition of being a man, the predictable responses followed, similar to those I'd received from the football players and the male college staffers. I forcefully (with some personal sadness and frustration) explained how amazingly loving, sensitive, vulnerable, and caring they were to voluntarily come out on a cold November evening to examine and challenge their understanding of masculinity. I said their desire to be better fathers to their sons was "lovely." Each man wasn't just being an "involved dad" but was also truly demonstrating themselves as "whole men" who were considering a new approach to being fathers, better fathers than the ones they'd had. I repeated these praises because they needed to truly hear it. Being a loving father is not just providing for our sons, but acting as these men were. We need to be accessible, exposed, and honest, showing our sons the same authentic, vulnerable love we want for ourselves.

In addition to teaching and nurturing in a deliberate way, men must model the qualities of what I call "joyful masculinity"—

fathering by embracing the vulnerability of expressing joy. Modeling happiness and love passes down happiness and love. We pass on the love of our favorite sports teams to our children not because we decorate their bedrooms with propaganda and memorabilia, but because they observe what makes us happy and brings us joy. Sometimes the joy, like that demonstrated by the dads that evening, is learning how to be a better father. In the example of my own father, it manifested in him learning the sports we played so he could play with us. The most distinct behaviors my father passed to me were those that brought him joy—those subtle delights that may be less obvious but are no less profound, and that are not governed by the performance of masculinity or directly in service to children.

Each time I sat down to work on this book, I had jazz pianist Keith Jarrett playing in the background because I have vivid recollections of the peace his music gave my father. I knew and appreciated the things he had to do to provide for us, but I also loved the things he wanted to do that were not about us.

BILL MAXWELL

Bill Maxwell was my quarterback coach in college. He was a masterful teacher, always positive and enthusiastic. In the "coaching" moments that required him to explain something in detail to me, his tone softened and he spoke in simple, unambiguous terms. I also spent a significant amount of time with Bill off the field. In addition to our endless football meetings, there was plenty of downtime on the road and at promotional events, as well as in countless impromptu meetings in his office, when the conversation strayed from football to academics, family, and life goals beyond college. The man I encountered in those times was forthrightly kind. It was a no-nonsense kindness, the sort necessary to nurture and support college football players who were balancing their bravado with a secret insecurity they hid behind a mask. What I marveled most about Bill Maxwell and what has remained in my memory after long-forgotten lessons of the game was his incredible generosity, patience, and respect. He was the first person who taught me that respect is given and not earned. I watched as he gave the custodian the same deference as he gave the university chancellor. He was never condescending and was uncommonly patient. The world around him was like crabs in a bucket and, unwaveringly, he was not. Bill was authentic. His gentle presence, juxtaposed with the environment of big-time college football, was conspicuous. His loving humanity and welcoming demeanor was not "tolerated" or "excused" by his coaching peers or the athletes he coached. It was cherished. His presence fostered an environment around him that was freed by his example from the mandate of masculinity.

Bill Maxwell was also meticulously organized. It was a necessary trait for a college quarterback coach. His notes were cogent, his penmanship perfectly legible, and he used colored pens to organize and highlight every game plan. This was consistent with his overall steady and contemplative demeanor. Honestly, I rarely gave Coach Maxwell's style much thought. He neither expected nor suggested that we (the other quarterbacks and I) adopt his approach. In fact, it was not until he passed away that I truly considered his subtle yet lasting influence.

My days in the NFL were completely uneventful. I never became a starter or even a regular player. But as a quarterback, I was still required to submit a game plan—the list of plays I felt comfortable executing according to the game's situations. Since my playing time was not a priority for the coaching staff, I was left to my own devices to organize my plan. Naturally, before my first professional game, my first stop was an office supply store to buy a set of colored pens. I did so for each of the seven years I played professional football, the last set purchased from a small card store somewhere just south of Montreal prior to the training camp of my final year. Even though my heart was no longer in the game, Bill Maxwell was in my heart.

When Bill passed away in 1998, I attended his funeral with those pens in my pocket. Grieving his death, and without adequate words to express what he meant to my life, I grabbed a symbol, a physical representation of how his life had influenced mine. The utility of the pens in that moment revealed to me what I was incapable of articulating: his example as a loving, kind, and gentle man was not just something to which I aspired as a twenty-two-year-old college student; he also provided me with a game plan on how to live my life.

The most profound and lasting qualities I took from Bill Maxwell were those I had consistently observed. There have been other men who have had a tremendous impact on my life. Similarly, their impact on me has been rooted in their observable behavior. Spoken and written words have inspired me and informed the philosophies that have guided my life, but my behaviors have been most influenced by watching men for whom I have great respect and admiration and who possess the qualities to which I aspire.

The journey I have been on since 1994, deconstructing masculinity and engaging men and boys in the work to end all forms of men's violence against women, has been personally transformative. It began with an awakening facilitated by the amazing survivors, advocates, and educators who opened my eyes and heart. The innumerable individuals who made up each audience fueled my resolve with their willingness to courageously delve into the issues, traversing the pain and distress that often come with growth and progress. The young men who have demonstrated what whole and healthy masculinity looks like have given me inspiration and hope for the future.

I LOVE YOU, MAN

In the final years of my father's life, he and my brothers and I shared more "I love yous" than we did in the entire preceding forty years of my life. Caring, sensitive, and vulnerable, we put aside the performance of men—fathers and sons—and were guided by our loving humanity. I fully recognize the amazing blessing it was to have that. It also made clearer the profound controlling power of the mandate of masculinity that had made the absence of that demonstrative love normal and okay.

It's often said that masculinity is in a state of crisis, that the paradigm governing the lives of boys and men is misleading and perilous. Perhaps this is true, as so much violence and social discontent stem from the aggressive defense of patriarchal values. And male privilege continues to keep us from seeing the destructive nature of living with only a portion of our wholeness and humanity.

But the real crisis is in the relationships we have with each other, and that begins with men and boys. Workshops, lectures, campaigns, slogans, and public-service messages will do nothing without the full engagement of fathers and men who serve as true role models and daily examples for boys. Boys not only aspire to emulate us; they have no choice but to become us. As the world around us evolves, so too must our understanding of what it means to be a man: a real man, a whole man, helping boys navigate our rapidly changing world. And while change can feel abrupt and scary, we must choose to be part of a transformative process. This is an amazing time and opportunity in our cultural history as adult men to be immersed in the process of teaching boys how to live in their wholeness, by courageously revealing and modeling our own whole humanity.

Acknowledgments

Thank you to the "angels and warriors" who serve those impacted by violence every day, and who do so in a world seemingly indifferent to the pain.

Thank you to the survivors, advocates, and educators who have edified my journey, allowed me the space to be wrong and the opportunity to serve—through your grace I have and will continue to learn and grow.

Thank you to Jessica Powers and Brian Baughan for your tireless work, patience, and guidance.